‘WESTERN W

The R C ‘Dick’ Riley Archive 1937 - 1964: Vol 1
Compiled by Jeremy Clements

The Transport Treasury

ISBN 978-1-913251-00-0

First Published in 2019 by Transport Treasury Publishing Ltd. 16 Highworth Close, High Wycombe, HP13 7PJ

www.ttpublishing.co.uk

Printed in the UK by Messrs. Henry Ling Ltd. Dorchester.

Contents

	Introduction	4
1	The Pre-war Great Western	7
2	Locomotives	15
3	Non-steam power	33
4	Coaches	41
5	Locations	51
6	Motive power depots	67
7	Signal boxes	73
8	Trains	85
9	Auto Trains	105
	Afterword	111

Front cover: Ready for their next turns, No 6020 *King Henry IV* and No 4088 *Dartmouth Castle* are recorded at Ranelagh Bridge. All the King Class 4-6-0s were fitted with double chimneys between September 1955 and December 1958. No 6020 was so treated in February 1956. This view was taken on 27th September 1958 and shows this engine (then allocated to Wolverhampton Stafford Road) to have the unique bogie with slotted front stretcher that was also associated with Nos 6004, 6023 and 6028. Partially out of shot is No 4088 which had been fitted with a double chimney in May of that year. Sixty-five Castles received this modification that included installation of higher degree superheating. The double chimney programme was very successful, resulting in substantially improved performances at modest cost. The winter 1958 timetable started on 11th September that year. Both locomotives have been turned for their next duties yet the King still carries Reporting Number 085 denoting the 7.30 am Mon-Sat Shrewsbury-Paddington. *RCR 12795.*

Title page: Class 68xx No 6826 *Nannerth Grange* basks in the sun at Long Rock, Penzance on 29th April 1961 with No 6814 *Enborne Grange* standing behind. This widely respected class was well suited to coping with the Devon and Cornwall switchback. The smart condition of this pair belies the sad reality that the glorious Indian Summer for Great Western steam was about to draw to a close. *RCR 15650.*

Opposite: Bogie repairs having been completed - *see page 25* - No 6001 *King Edward V11* was at Old Oak Common on 5th May 1956. The reporting number chalked on the smokebox suggests that it had last been employed on the 6.45 am Wolverhampton-Paddington service. *RCR 5948.*

Rear cover: Indoors at Old Oak Common. *RCR 8268.*

Introduction

There is always pleasure in studying the work of a master craftsman, the more so when he is an accomplished railway photographer, and above all when his camera is aimed at the Great Western Railway. Dick Riley travelled extensively throughout the United Kingdom to capture the pageantry on film. In the process he developed a particular affiliation with Swindon's products although his earliest railway experiences were apparently engaged in the activities of the "other" companies.

Brought up in the Dulwich area, he attended school in central London which meant a daily return journey to Holborn Viaduct. This was the natural habitat of ex-South Eastern & Chatham Railway motive power enrichened by that of the Midland and Great Northern railways, courtesy of the City Widened Lines and the Snow Hill Tunnel. His first attempts at railway photography were at Kings Cross which quickly revealed the limitations of the Box Brownie, and led to a more sophisticated Kodak camera. The quality of his work immediately improved although inadequate shutter speeds prevented capture of trains on the move. This was of little consequence for his artistic eye was clearly developing and while the subject matter might be static, his focus was on locomotives of inherent historic interest. Some of these received life extensions due to wartime demands but did not survive for long thereafter.

How and why interest developed in the GWR is not recorded but it may well have been stimulated by school trips which were common before the war, and from the late 1940s on into the 1960s. This was a time before the concept of public liability assumed today's draconian dimensions. The railway authorities were content to grant official permission for enthusiasts to visit locomotive depots, perhaps as an aid to personnel recruitment later, and visitors in gratitude for the privilege behaved themselves. Certainly, many of the early photographs in the Collection were taken inside the fence meaning that Dick Riley must have been a regular participant in such events.

After the war, he worked in banking. Because the industry then opened to the public on Saturday mornings, he could not visit London termini to witness the plethora of departures to summer holiday destinations. In compensation, good use was made of family holidays in the West Country which is why views of the Paddington-Bristol-Plymouth-Penzance thread feature so prominently. Dick Riley visited Plymouth in March 1938 and he made at least eleven more trips to that city between July 1955 and July 1963. On six occasions he went further west, to St Blazey and beyond. Also, rather than restrict himself to specific centres, he toured extensively through the local countryside to record the railway in various rural settings.

For coverage of multiple locations within a limited space of time, he relied on his Morris Minor Tourer ("convertible" in modern parlance). More detail about this car is included in *Afterword* but suffice to say here that its performance was modest at best. In itself, this would not have been a major impediment in those pre-motorway times given the condition of the road network, and the scarcity of by-passes to avoid towns and cities. Average speeds were low and could turn a 200-mile journey into an expedition lasting more than six hours. Summer journey times were even worse in the West Country, a major tourist destination before the advent of the overseas package holiday.

The results of Dick Riley's dedication to long distance travel in fulfilment of his artistry are contained within a photographic collection estimated at 18,000 black-and-white images. Initial selection for this work took place at editorial level to isolate in the main those most appropriate to the more southerly reaches of the Great Western's world, hopefully to leave other areas for later attention. The specific choice of which should be included or omitted in this volume was left to the compiler – a challenge in view of the amount of material, but intensely enjoyable.

In the preparation of captions, particular attention

has been paid to train composition where appropriate. All too often commentaries in books and contemporary steam-related magazines concentrate on motive power while paying scant attention to what the locomotive is hauling. By the mid-1960s, trains in the west were bland and only late surviving Sunshine or Hawksworth stock lurking within the Mark 1 armada provided interest (and of course the vehicle of choice in which to ride). So, let Dick Riley take the reader back to those treasured earlier years of cluttered diversity when fascination lay in locomotives, coaches, wagons, signals and much, much more.

Jeremy Clements, Co Meath 2019.

Unfulfilled visions of a modern Great Western are reflected in this view of Express Parcels Diesel-Mechanical Railcar No W34W switching from the Down Slow on arrival at Southall, with a Fruit D and an ex-LMS Passenger Brake Van in tow. Rather more traditional is 2-6-2T Class 61xx No 6126 shunting wagons behind. Two forms of Great Western motive power immutably associated with the London Division. ***RCR 11078***

This early example of Dick Riley's work shows two generations of moguls at Worcester on 12th March 1939. Prominent is Class 26xx No 2679 which might be described as the freight version of *City of Truro.* This unusual design was introduced by William Dean in 1900 and eventually totalled 81 locomotives. Earlier examples carried a variety of boilers in an experiment to determine the optimal type before settling on the now familiar tapered Standard No 4. These engines were known by their "Aberdare" nickname following their concentration on Aberdare-Swindon heavy coal trains when first introduced. They remained in mineral and freight haulage, and were very rarely seen on passenger trains.

They had 4' 7½" driving wheels so the combination of low running plate and high footplate imparted an impression of height and power when looking forward from the cab. They ran initially with 3500-gallon tenders (and briefly with some of the few Churchward 4000-gallon variety) but from the 1930s onwards many acquired 4000-gallon tenders of Great Central design origin, as with No 2579 here. These tenders had arrived on the GWR with war surplus ROD 2-8-0s and were re-deployed following withdrawal of their companion locomotives. Withdrawal of Aberdares started in 1934 but their working lives were extended by the demands of war (five taken out of service in 1939 were placed in store and later returned to duty). Only twelve survived to become British Railways property. No 2679, the penultimate class member built in 1902 was withdrawn in November 1946.

The Churchward era is exemplified by the Class 43xx 2-6-0 standing behind the Aberdare. The casting mounted behind the buffer beam indicates that this was one of 65 engines of the 53xx series to be modified in this fashion. The purpose was to increase the weight borne by the pony wheels by about two tons and thereby exert more side thrust on the main frames. This reduced flange wear on the leading driving wheels, one of the two main drawbacks to a useful mixed traffic design (the other was a tendency to roll at higher speeds). The casting modification was not elegant but it worked, except that it elevated the engine's route availability from blue to red category. Following withdrawal of older 4-4-0s used on blue routes, the castings were removed and the original availability was restored. For the period that the castings were in place, the locomotives concerned were renumbered in the 83xx series. *RCR 149.*

Chapter 1

Pre-war

It is uncertain precisely when Dick Riley started to take photographs of railway subjects as many early images in the Collection are undated, but it seems to have been around 1937. The quality of these early views does not match his later work for two understandable reasons. Firstly, he stated many years later that he did not regard his work as fully matured until about 1954 for reasons touched on in the Introduction. Secondly, his pre-war camera equipment had slow shutter speeds that confined him to static subjects. Nevertheless, his eye for ageing and obscure locomotives led him to capture some whose extinction was imminent. On those grounds alone, these early efforts deserve inclusion in this work.

Dick Riley seems to have roamed far and wide as

Tyseley was visited on 25th June 1939 and the collection contains at least three photographs of large prairies taken that day. No 5125 was built as 3125 in May 1905, following the success of the experimental prototype No 99 of 1903 (later No 3100, then No 5100, and finally its frames went to the new No 8100 in 1938). No 3125 was superheated from May 1905, and in about 1909 received the support struts between smokebox and buffer beam. This latter measure was to relieve pressure on the frames when banking trains; the engine's other duties were typically mixed traffic in nature. The only other change evident is the fitting of a lower cab roof while the original tall style safety valve bonnet remains. A few of the class received curved front footplates and outside steam pipes but No 5125 remained unchanged in this respect until withdrawal in July 1952. The original 40 built between 1903 and 1906 proved sufficient for the company's needs until construction in essentially unchanged form resumed in 1929. Eventually 140 more were delivered between then and December 1949. No 3125 was renumbered in November 1928 to co-ordinate with the number series applied to the new engines that were introduced from the following year. The first forty engines had been distributed widely throughout the GWR system but with the arrival of the new locomotives from 1929 onwards, they were concentrated mainly in the Wolverhampton Division. In 1938, thirty-four of the ex-31xx series were based in the area. ***RCR 192***

visits included Plymouth Laira, Severn Tunnel Junction, Taunton, Tyseley, Worcester. Inevitably Swindon was on the list, a wonderful place to visit in the days of steam, overwhelming in the amount of "Great Westernry" on display, and exciting in the anticipated discovery of rare gems in quiet corners. Official supervision was avuncular, relaxed and friendly. "Health" was imparted by the sheer pleasure of indulgence in mankind's greatest free entertainment show. "Safety" was an entirely separate concept driven by basic common sense.

Albums usually commence by focussing on glamour locomotives but it seems appropriate on this occasion to start with some of the ageing and lesser machines that excited his attention.

During the 19th Century there was a dichotomy between Swindon and Wolverhampton in the design and construction of four-coupled passenger tank locomotives. The Northern Division favoured 0-4-2Ts of the Class 517 family while Swindon preferred the "Metropolitan" 2-4-0Ts; both types were built over long periods in considerable numbers with a resultant variety in size, cabs, tanks etc. The nickname, colloquially shortened to "Metro", was based on their use on services over the Metropolitan Railway via Baker Street and the City Widened Lines. These included passenger services up until 1907 but condenser-fitted Metros, minus cab roofs continued on Smithfield meat trains until displaced by 97xx pannier tanks. Metros came in three basic sizes and No 3581 is readily identifiable as one of the large variety by virtue of the volute springs over the leading axle. This view was taken at Taunton while hauling an auto trailer and is undated but likely to have been taken in 1938/9. This locomotive was withdrawn in November 1945.
RCR 530.

Top: More modern motive power did not escape attention. 0-6-2T Class 56xx No 5625 was in the shed yard at Severn Tunnel Junction on 14th April 1938. Apart from the smokebox stains, this engine was in smart condition – a marked contrast to STJ's contingent of Class 3150s which were preferred for banking duties through the tunnel, and were constantly filthy as a result. *RCR 258.*

Middle: Bird series Bulldog No 3452 *Penguin* less its tender was awaiting attention at Swindon works on 27th November 1938. *RCR 102.*

Bottom: Introduced in 1874, Wolverhampton-built 0-6-0ST Class 850 eventually totalled 170 locomotives that penetrated virtually every corner of the GWR. Its modest axle loading allowed a broad measure of utility, which was greatly aided by a surprising power output in relation to its diminutive size. No 2001 was built in December 1891, converted to pannier tank in August 1911, and withdrawn in August 1952. The view was taken at Worcester in March 1939. *RCR 144.*

This page: The last 15 of the Bulldog Class were named after birds, and were immediately recognisable by their deeper outside frames. No 3441 *Blackbird* was at Plymouth Laira shed in August 1937 and most probably engaged in piloting heavy trains over the South Devon banks. The 3500-gallon tender with the Collett-era continuous pattern fender more readily associated with Halls, Granges and Saints appears incongruous. *RCR 282.*

Opposite top: Introduced in 1870, Swindon-built 0-6-0ST Class 1076 (nicknamed "Buffalo") was associated mainly, but not exclusively, with the GWR's Southern Division and in its early years was engaged on long distance freight duties. This was a popular type made distinctive by the outside frames; the majority in due course had their saddle tanks replaced with the more familiar panniers. They were particularly smooth running engines and for this reason later found favour on auto train services. By the late 1930s, few remained of a class that had once totalled 266. Built in April 1900 and converted to pannier tank in November 1917, No 1620 engaged in shunting at Swindon on 6th April 1938 was an obvious target for Dick Riley's camera. Unlike much of his early work, this image is specifically dated which presents a problem as records show this engine to have been withdrawn in November 1937. Either the photograph's date is an error or despite the order for withdrawal, there was a reluctance to say good-bye to this grand old veteran so its career was eked out by use on departmental-type duties. It is nice to believe that the photographer did not make a mistake with the date. *RCR 232.*

Opposite bottom: Another veteran tank locomotive appears in this pre-war but undated photograph. Wolverhampton-built 0-4-2T No 1442 (not to be confused with the Class 14xx of the same number that resides in Tiverton Museum) was a relatively late example (built January 1878) of the large and heterogeneous Class 517 that first appeared in April 1868. No 1442 was one of the last six in service being allocated to Swindon at withdrawal in May 1945. To the left of the 0-4-2T stands an ex-ROD 2-8-0 of Class 30xx. This locomotive has been fitted with GWR-style top feed but retains the smokebox door and elegant Robinson chimney that betray its Great Central design origins. To the rear stands a Loco coal wagon. The GWR was a major shipper of coal for its own account (eg Old Oak Common shed accepted 3000 tons per week) and had recognised years earlier that the economics strongly favoured 20-ton 4-wheel and 40-ton bogie wagons. Nevertheless, the wagon depicted was a low capacity vehicle of which significant numbers remained at work. In this case, the capacity has been increased by an extension affixed to the iron body. *RCR 241.*

Above: Another strange locomotive and tender pairing concerned Duke Class 4-4-0 No 3284 *Isle of Jersey* seen at Tyseley on 25th June 1939. When introduced in 1895, this class was closely associated with services west of Newton Abbot where short turntables dictated the use of diminutive 2000-gallon tenders. Now this engine has a 3500-gallon tender with long fenders that looks distinctly out of place. No 3284 (as No 9084) was the last but one member of the class at work being withdrawn in April 1951 after 52 years' service. *RCR 291.*

Opposite: 2-4-0T crane tank No 1299 had an unusual history. When the South Devon Railway was taken over by the Great Western on 1st February 1876, there were three broad gauge 2-4-0STs under construction at Newton Abbot works. The partially completed locomotives (intended to be named *Saturn*, *Jupiter*, and *Mercury*) were removed to Swindon for completion; a young SDR employee named Churchward who hailed from the village of Stoke Gabriel on the River Dart was also transferred to Swindon around this time.

The trio duly emerged in December 1878, having been converted to narrow (i.e. "standard") gauge 2-4-0 side tanks, identified by the numbers 1298 to 1300. A typical branch line locomotive of the late 19th Century, No 1299 was converted to a crane tank in April 1881 and allocated to the Engineering Department at Reading where it remained until June 1893. It then reverted to ordinary stock while retaining the lifting equipment, and then become Departmental Stock in May 1925. The date of its move to Swindon is unknown but the exercise must have required the crane to be dismantled as the boom could apparently only be rotated and so exceeded the loading gauge.

Crane tanks were favoured for fetching and carrying materials around locomotive works and the GWR had three purpose-built 0-6-4T examples. These were based on the pannier tank version of 0-6-0 Class 850 with an extended platform at the rear to carry the crane. In this case, the boom could be both rotated and raised, with a maximum load capacity of 9 tons, which is likely to have exceeded anything that No 1299 could manage. The three were: No 16 *Hercules* (built April 1921 and always a Swindon engine), No 17 *Cyclops* (built April 1901 and for a time at Stafford Road, Wolverhampton before return to Swindon) and No 18 *Steropes* (built April 1901 and believed always to have been at Swindon). With advances in other methods of materials handling, the crane tanks gradually became redundant and all four were withdrawn in September 1936. They stood for over a year in Swindon yard before being broken up.

This 1937 photograph must have been one of Dick Riley's earliest, given the sequence of events described above. No 1299 was standing between two of the 0-6-4PT crane tanks as their counterbalance weights are visible at either side of the photograph. *RCR Ref unconfirmed.*

Pre-war

The military authorities, recalling the sterling service rendered by 62 Dean Goods in 1917-9 in France and later Greece, requested the loan of 100 of the type shortly after the outbreak of war in 1939, and a further eight followed in early 1940. At the fall of France in May-June 1940, the 79 by then in that country supporting the British Expeditionary Force were abandoned to their fate and most were taken over by the French and German railway authorities. With no reasonable expectation of their early recovery, the Government officially purchased all 108 in October 1940. By the time of the Liberation of Europe the class was scattered far and wide but a number were recovered and returned to British military service. Following restoration of peace, it was determined that wherever feasible the survivors should be repatriated although those in operable condition did remain on a temporary basis with French railways which were short of motive power.

The condition of many was by then appalling and all were closely inspected on arrival at Dover. Some, judged unsafe to be moved further, were scrapped on the spot while others were despatched direct to breakers. The economics of this exercise might seem curious but there was an acute shortage of scrap metal in Britain at the time.

It has not been possible to identify the locomotive in this undated photograph but the location is Longmoor. The tender to the rear is marked LMR (for "Longmoor Military Railway") and probably relates to one of the Riddles-designed WD 2-10-0s working on that system. Dean Goods WD No 70195 (ex-GWR No 2531) was the very last of the type to remain "in service" being used for training in re-railing techniques up until 1959 but it has not been possible to confirm whether this is the locomotive depicted. Nevertheless, the view gives of good impression of the condition to which many of those brought home had been reduced. *RCR 12854.*

Chapter 2

Locomotives

Post war, Dick Riley continued to pay attention to those elements of the motive power fleet whose age threatened impending obsolescence. Saints and Stars, diminishing breeds by that time, came into focus and heightened interest in a drab and tired railway system that so typified the peacetime austerity years. Gradually as the veterans melted away, there was a renaissance in locomotive liveries. Lined green could always be expected with 4-6-0s but its appearance on other types that worked passenger trains was a welcome development which heralded steam's Indian summer on the Western Region. This policy embraced some mixed traffic 2-8-0s and tank locomotives that had only qualified for unlined mid-chrome green under previous ownership. This was evidence of a management team deeply conscious of what the "Great Western Region" had inherited, and determined to celebrate the legacy.

Military service in both world wars led to William Dean's 0-6-0 Class 2301 (the "Dean Goods") becoming the most widely travelled of all GWR types. These classically late-Victorian, modestly-sized locomotives eventually saw service in continental Europe, North Africa and China earning widespread respect for their versatility and efficiency. One Italian driver remarked that the "Churchills", as they were known in wartime Europe, were "small but very strong". No 2431, built in 1893, was one of those that served only on the home front. It was allocated to Carmarthen where it was photographed on 9th September 1951. Its poor external condition suggests that it was near the end of its working career and indeed withdrawal came the following November. ***RCR 3446.***

Dean Goods No 2466, built in January 1896, was lent to the government in 1939 becoming WD No 179 (and sold in October 1940). It was one of the 29 that stayed at home, working for the army mainly in the south of England. Whereas other class members sent to France in great haste received minimal modifications, this engine was one of ten that was given more thorough attention.

It was fitted with pannier tanks that extended from the cab front to a point slightly to the rear of the leading axle. The tanks were deep, the upper edge being flush with the boiler top and the lower edge just clearing the splashers. They stood proud of the cab and in line with the outer edge of the running plate. The tanks were fitted with the GWR's standard condensing gear. Westinghouse brakes were also installed, with the pump mounted on the right-hand side of the smokebox and a pair of air cylinders set vertically on the left.

The tanks and condensing equipment were a tight squeeze that compromised the low axle loading but intended to increase operating range where water supplies were inadequate and to reduce steam emission that could betray the locomotive's presence to hostile elements. This equipment does not seem to have been ever used although the engine was photographed in this condition while helping in Tank Landing Craft loading rehearsals prior to the D-Day landings. When photographed at Longmoor on 25th May 1946 as No 70179, the tanks and condensing gear had been removed, and the air cylinder re-positioned horizontally just ahead of the cab while the Westinghouse pump remained in situ.

This engine finally saw foreign service shortly after this photograph was taken. In 1946/ 7, the United Nations Relief and Rehabilitation Administration sent 25 operational members of the class plus a donor for spares to China. Twenty-two still working in France were sent direct and the remainder, including No 70179, were supplied by the War Department from its UK-based fleet. No record has been traced of their subsequent careers as China was embroiled in bitter civil war at the time. *RCR 1215.*

Those in authority at British Railways Western Region were aware of vanishing GWR locomotive heritage in the 1950s and took measures to save 4-6-0 Star Class No 4003 *Lode Star* and Dean Goods No 2516, now both part of the National Collection. Enthusiasts recognised that Churchward's Saint Class was equally significant and pleaded in vain for the last survivor, No 2920 *St David*, to be saved on withdrawal in October 1953. Happily, this significant omission has been rectified by sterling efforts within the preservation community, resulting in "new" No 2999 *Lady of Legend.*

Another worthy candidate would have been No 2906 *Lady of Lynn* which was in a partially modernised condition when photographed at Cardiff Canton, its home shed, in May 1952. When introduced, the first Churchward 4-6-0s were criticised for their stark, angular appearance which was at odds with the elegant styling of other Edwardian designs. More importantly, they were fitted with lever (pole) reverse which had no capacity for fine adjustment as was possible with screw reverse.

When fitted with new cylinders in October 1935, the more stylish curved drop end at the front was installed (in all, five of the "Ladies" series were so treated). No change was made to the drop end at the rear (nor to the lever reverse) resulting in a hybrid style. *Lady of Lynn* was withdrawn in August 1952 after a working career of a little over 46 years. *RCR 3563.*

Opposite page: At the end of 1897, there were 213 locomotives of the 2-4-0 wheel arrangement in service with the GWR, the third most numerous after the fleets of 0-6-0s and 0-6-0Ts. Thereafter, numbers steadily declined and the last GW-built examples (Nos 3210 and 3222 of the sandwich-framed "Barnum" Class) were withdrawn in March 1937, leaving only Nos 1334 to 1336 in service. These had been built by Dübs & Co for the Midland & South Western Junction Railway in 1894 to work through passenger and mail services. After the Grouping, Swindon seemed to take a shine to ex-MSWJR locomotives and several were rebuilt. In the case of the 2-4-0s, they were all "westernised" by the fitting of Standard No 11 boilers in 1924. Their activities were then centred on lighter duties in the Didcot/ Reading area with particular emphasis on Lambourn line services.

Their age and by then rare wheel arrangement gave them a measure of celebrity in the early 1950s, and they were called upon to work enthusiasts' specials. Nos 1334/ 5 were withdrawn in September 1952 while No 1336 soldiered on until March 1954. Two views depict these quaint little engines in their closing years. No 1335, the only one to receive a BR smokebox number plate (while retaining the old-fashioned smokebox door) is shown at Reading shed in May 1951. At the same location No 1336 has lost its crank axle and buffers but had acquired a more modern smokebox door while retaining its buffer beam identity. *RCR 3150 / 3153.*

Above: Another late surviving Churchward 4-6-0 was Star Class No 4062 *Malmesbury Abbey* which had been built in May 1922, seen at what is believed was Swindon shed on 15th June 1952. No 4062 was fitted in March 1950 with the unusual "elbow" outside steam pipes which doubled back behind the frames. This became necessary with the installation of new inside cylinders or saddle while retaining the original outside cylinders. Where new outside cylinders were also installed, Castle-type steam pipes were applied. The coupling of a Hawksworth 4000-gallon flat sided, welded tender was possibly a unique partnership. This type first appeared with the 4-6-0 Counties, and in slightly narrower form worked with Castles, Halls and Modified Halls. *RCR 3685.*

BRITISH RAILWAYS
4056
PRINCESS MARGARET

Opposite top: The last Churchward-built 4-6-0 in service was Star Class No 4056 *Princess Margaret*, a Bristol Bath Road engine and something of a shed "pet" in the months before withdrawal in October 1957. Like No 4062, this engine has acquired the distinctive "elbow" outside steam pipes (in August 1949) but is running with a more appropriate Collett 4000-gallon tender. It was photographed at Old Oak Common on 23rd September 1956 in company with No 7032 *Denbigh Castle* which survived until September 1964. *RCR 7998.*

Opposite bottom: A view of No 4056's cab taken from the tender at Old Oak Common on 23rd September 1956. An unidentified Castle stands to the left and No 7027 *Thornbury Castle* is on the right. *RCR 8000.*

This page: Another worthy representative of earlier times was 4-4-0 Class 90xx No 9017, one of the last two examples of GWR double-framed 4-4-0 in ordinary service. A creation of the 1930's where a lighter Duke type boiler was mounted on a Bulldog chassis to increase route availability, this class harked back directly to William Dean and the GWR's golden years at the turn of the century. Dick Riley obviously knew what was about to be lost as he took several photographs of this grand old engine at Llwyngwril, Vriog, Fairbourne, Barmouth, Criccieth, Pwllhei as well here at Dovey Junction, and all on 30th September 1960. The date is significant as Nos 9017 was withdrawn the following month, but has fortunately survived in preservation. *RCR 15432.*

One of the operating advantages enjoyed by the venerable Dean Goods was its uncoloured route availability whereas its nominal successor, Collett's Class 2251, was in the yellow category. Nevertheless, the more modern type was spread throughout the GWR system on a multiplicity of secondary duties. No 3201, built in September 1946, was seen at Bala Junction on 27th July 1951 coupled to an older vintage tender. *RCR 3293.*

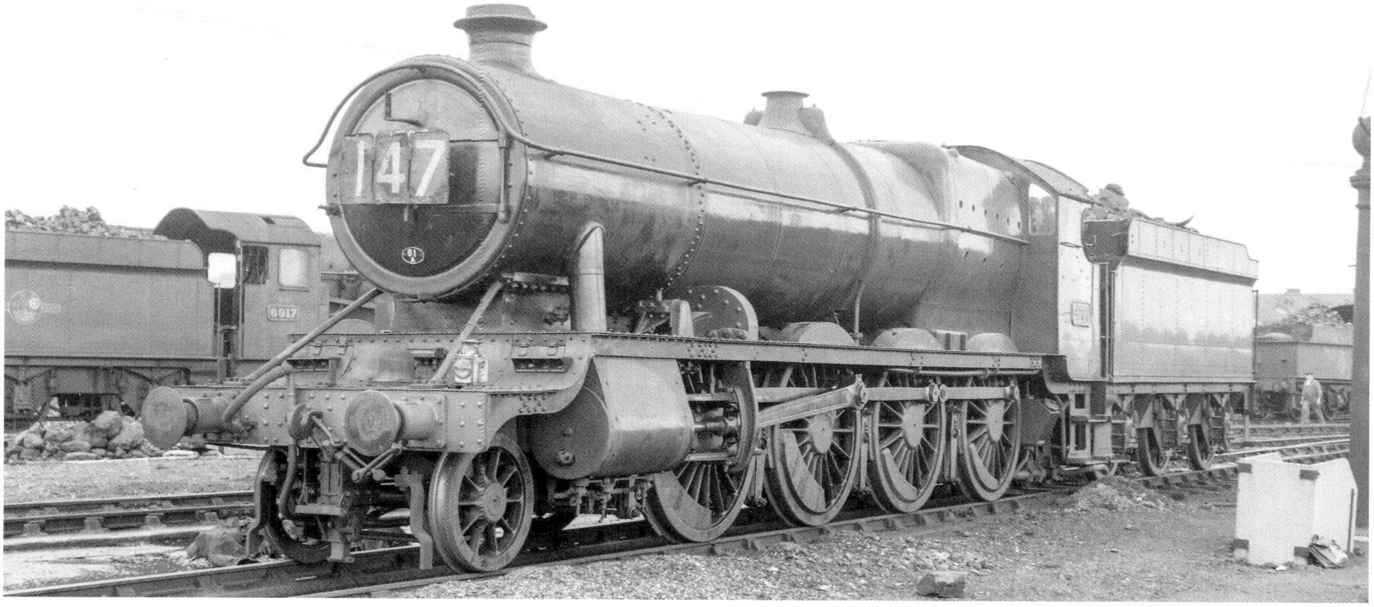

Churchward's final design was 2-8-0 Class 47xx. The first appeared in May 1919 and was fitted with a Standard No 1 boiler which proved inadequate to cope with its intended duties on long distance fitted freight services. Two years later, the purpose-designed larger Standard No 7 boiler was installed and in this form, No 4700 and the eight that followed proved very effective. These large 2-8-0s were most imposing machines and the appearance of prototype No 4700 seen here at Old Oak Common on 10th August 1957 was enhanced by its lined green livery. In their later years, they fulfilled their mixed traffic role by hauling all but the fastest passenger trains; the train reporting number refers to the 12.05 pm Saturdays only Paddington-Plymouth. The locomotive behind is No 6017 *King Edward IV. RCR 11062.*

The crew of sparkling Class 47xx No 4705 await the "right away" on 13th May 1961 from Steventon on what is probably a Swindon-bound local train from Reading or Didcot. Along with a Swindon to Bristol service, this was a regular running-in turn. *RCR 15745.*

Top: Getting late in its career, 28xx No 2883 basks in the sun at Tyseley on 28th May 1960. Beneath the grime the presence of the "Ferret & Dart Board" on the tender shows that this locomotive has received a repaint during the previous three years. No 2883 was built in April 1919 as the last of the Churchward version of this much-respected class. From the following year, additional heavy freight demands were met by purchases of war-surplus ROD 2-8-0s (Class 30xx). Construction of the 28xx type, in the form of the 2884 side-window cab version, re-commenced in April 1938. *RCR 14764.*

Bottom: On 12th March 1955, Class 43xx 2-6-0 No 5368 reverses away from Old Oak Common in the direction of Paddington with the incline towards the flying junction in the background. The purpose of this trip was most likely to gain access to one of the groups of sidings to the south of the main line in the OOC area. *RCR 5678.*

Among the 8P locomotives acquired by British Railways, the 4-6-0 Kings were unique in being used solely on top link passenger services (apart from running-in turns), unlike Gresley, Stanier and Bulleid pacifics that were found on secondary duties in their declining years. This was partly due to their retention to handle increased London-Birmingham traffic diverted to the ex-GWR route during electrification of the southern portion of the West Coast Main Line.

In the mid-1950s and before that requirement emerged, the Kings were approaching 30 years of express service and beginning to show their age, most significantly in the condition of their bogies. Frames had suffered fatigue cracks from time to time in the past and repairs were usually satisfactorily effected by welding. However, in January 1956 the incidence of cracking sharply escalated, requiring more rigorous repair measures. The entire class was temporarily withdrawn and additional stiffening strips were welded to the frames, a solution that worked well. No 6012 was the first to return to service in early February and the remainder soon followed. No 6025 *King Henry III* is standing at Old Oak Common on 4th February 1956 with the bogie removed and the front end supported by jacks. No 6013 *King Henry VIII* is behind and a supporting jack can just be detected under its buffer beam. *RCR 5801.*

With the Kings temporarily out of commission for bogie repairs, Coronation and Princess Royal pacifics were borrowed from the London Midland Region to cover top link obligations. Coronation No 46237 *City of Bristol* has arrived at Paddington Platform 9 on 21st April 1956 with the 4.15 pm (Saturdays excepted) Bristol-Paddington. It was fortunate that the bogie problem occurred in mid-winter as the resultant disruption would have been more extreme during the summer months when WR and LMR demand for 8P motive power was intense. *RCR 6043.*

Class 72xx 2-8-2T No 7239 was standing in sidings at Oxford (Rewley Road) on 15th August 1959. The ex-LNWR signal box is to the right and the GWR's Oxford North Junction Signal Box is in the right background. *RCR 14095.*

Above: Lucky number? 0-6-0PT Class 57xx No 7777 in Worcester shed yard on 7th April 1958. This locomotive enjoyed a working life of precisely 30 years – into service November 1930 and withdrawn November 1960. *RCR 11552.*

Right: Class 57xx No 5723 had been reduced to the humble role of stationary boiler at a West London Yard, or possibly near the creosote works at Southall on 16th August 1958. *RCR 12612.*

Top: Originally intended as a shunting type in the 19th Century, the 0-6-0ST/ PT Class 2021 had evolved into a useful light passenger locomotive but by the 1930s it was ageing and becoming obsolete. The concept was therefore revived in three classes (54xx, 64xx and 74xx) of which the first two were equipped to operate auto trains. Introduced in 1932, a duty particularly associated with Class 64xx was the auto train service between Plymouth North Road and Saltash for which duty Laira shed typically maintained a contingent of eight. No 6400 is seen standing under the shear legs at the depot on 30th April 1961 while receiving attention to the rear axle set which has been removed; the rear end is supported by the pulley and tackle suspended from the overhead equipment. No 6400 is in lined green livery which was applied to many tank locomotives used on passenger work at that time.
RCR 15686.

This page: The Great Western favoured labelling their 4-6-0s with the private addresses of the nobility and gentry. This practice became rather tedious so "non-Castle" names on Castles made for a welcome change, giving distinction to the locomotives concerned. With the third (5098) series some evocative names with historic associations were selected:- *Viscount Portal, Sir James Milne, Sir Edward Elgar, Great Western, Swindon*, and certainly not least, *G.J. Churchward* (No 7017). It is a pity that C.B. Collett and F.W. Hawksworth were never so honoured. No 7017 was on display in the presence of admirers at Old Oak Common on 29th August 1959. *RCR 14208.*

Opposite middle: Class 57xx plus its later version with a modernised cab (the 8750 series) formed by far the most numerous class on the GWR. For the most part their appearance did not change much so installation of a spark arrester naturally attracted attention, as with No 3709 photographed at Truro shed on 2nd July 1960. This equipment was very likely needed for shunting the docks at Falmouth. The locomotive to the right is No 6870 *Bodicote Grange. RCR 15163.*

Opposite bottom: No 7925 *Westol Hall* awaits departure on an Up working from Par on 3rd September 1954. There is no train reporting number and the destination boards on the leading Brake Third coach have been reversed which suggests a return positioning working. The locomotive livery appears to be the early BR neo-LNWR mixed traffic style (i.e. red and white lining on a black background) with red backing to the number and nameplates. This looked striking when freshly painted but seemed to "go off" as grime set in. On the tender, the insignia "G coat of arms W" is just discernible and there is no evidence of lining suggesting that the wartime GWR economy livery was still in place. In the early BR years, it was not unusual for a green locomotive to be coupled to a black tender and *vice versa.* The driver's personal livery includes a stylish trilby – or possibly he is a locomotive inspector. *RCR 5399.*

4073

CO-OPERATIVE SERVICE
LCS
SOCIETY
LONDONERS LIKE IT
Panda
The PANDA
QUALITY DRY CLEANING AND LAUNDRY
SUPER DRY CLEANERS

Opposite: The transfer of No 4073 *Caerphilly Castle* to the Science Museum, South Kensington on 5th June 1961 was comprehensively photographed and the street scene with the Pickfords low loaders has appeared elsewhere. The view of the locomotive a couple of days before the move is less well-known and shows the engine protected from the elements inside the Pullman shed at Old Oak Common. It deserves close study for the extraordinary quality of the restoration that had been carried out at Swindon.
RCR 15797 & 15858.

Above: Construction of British Railways 2-10-0 Class 9F No 92220 was completed at Swindon in February 1960 and it was photographed in "A" Shop in plain black livery. Between then and the poignant ceremony held on 18th March 1960 at which the name *Evening Star* was unveiled, the significance of being the last steam locomotive built for British Railways was recognised through application of lined green livery, with the name depicted in the standard GWR font. The locomotive was photographed at Old Oak Common on 2nd April 1960. *RCR 14575.*

The first diesel-mechanical railcar entered service in December 1933 as a single suburban unit and by 1936, fifteen more had been added. Intended for longer distance duties, the later vehicles were more powerful and all shared the modernistic external styling, earning them the "Flying Banana" nickname. Nos 2 to 4 were specifically express units with first and third class sections, two toilets and catering facilities while Nos 5 to 16 were simpler in layout. The concept proved popular, often generating more custom than could be accommodated within a single vehicle, but absence of drawgear prevented attachment of a trailer.

Railcar No 17 as shown here was different in being intended solely for parcels traffic within the London area. Internally, apart from the guard's facilities, it was simply a van with no internal partitions except for those that closed off the driving cabs. Outwardly the body profile followed that of Railcars Nos 8 to 16 but without windows except in the sliding doors on each side. No 17 worked entirely satisfactorily from April 1936 until January 1959 and was photographed in store at Swindon. Sections of the side skirting below the sole bar had been removed to improve access to engines and transmission, to the detriment of the enveloping streamlined appearance. However, while several of the other units also lost the side shaft that coupled the bogie axles, in this case the original drive train remains. An unidentified passenger railcar stands behind No 17. *RCR Ref unconfirmed.*

The inability of the first seventeen diesel railcars to haul trailer vehicles was a significant operating limitation. Experimental car No 18 retained art deco exterior styling but was equipped with conventional buffers and drawgear. From No 19 onwards, a revised body type was adopted with razor edge styling to the driving cabs. Whereas the earlier railcars had been intended mostly for mainline express work, Nos 19 to 33 were essentially suburban or branch line units. In this undated view, No W22W is departing from Leamington. *RCR 10440.*

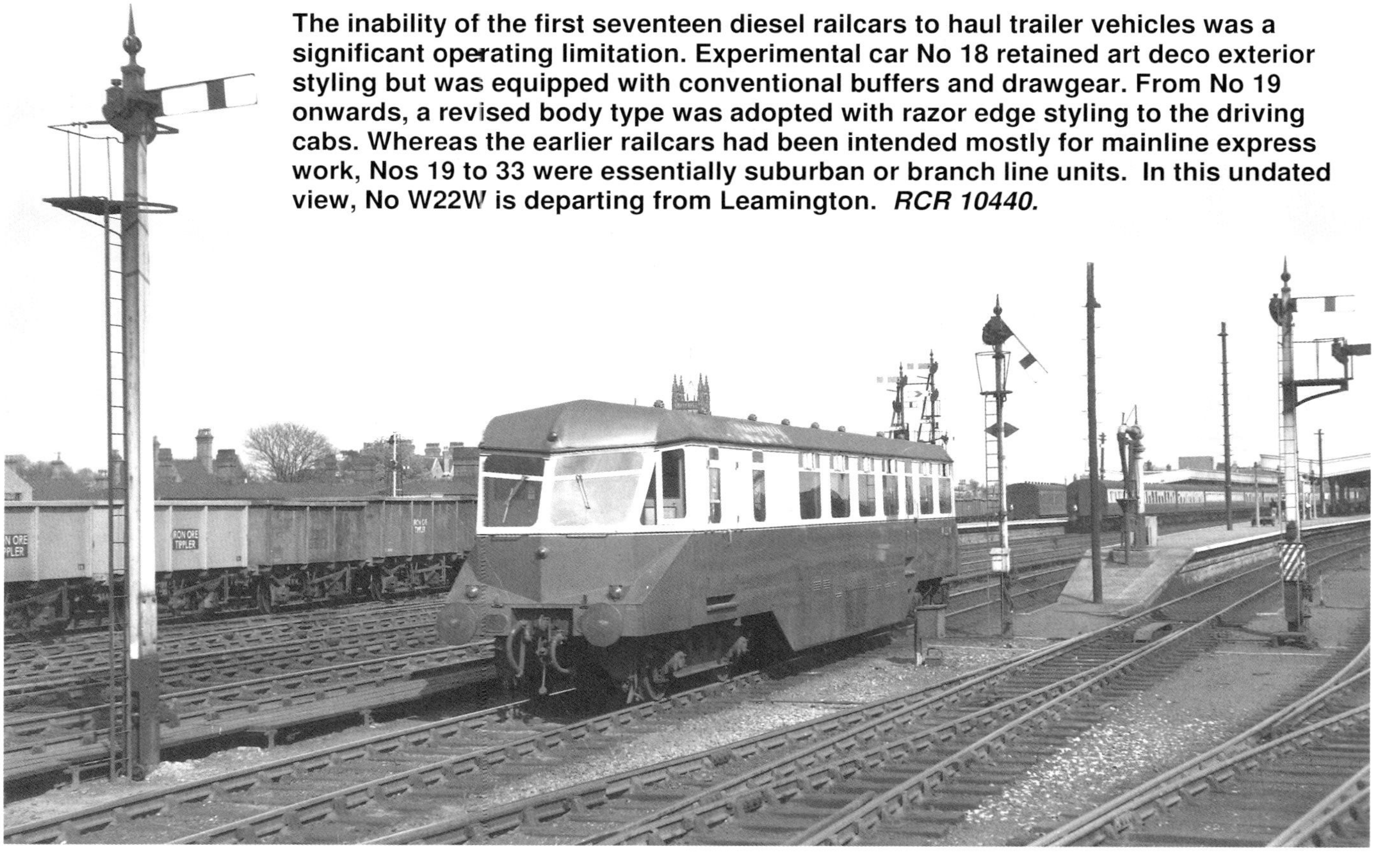

Chapter 3

Non-steam power

The Great Western was circumspect in its approach to electricity as a source of motive power. Mainline overhead electrification (Paddington to Bristol/ Birmingham plus Devon & Cornwall) was subjected to independent expert evaluation in 1925. Taunton-Penzance was reviewed again in 1938 but both studies concluded that projected investment returns did not justify the expense. In 1926/ 7, William Beardmore & Co submitted proposals for 4-coach diesel-electric trains of a style generally similar to British Railways' Hastings units; the GWR also studied the experimental DEMU tested by the LMS in the Blackpool-Preston area in 1928/ 9. These initiatives faded away following the departure of Felix Pole as General Manager.

Nevertheless, diesel power remained on the agenda and took shape in the railcar fleet that exploited technically simpler diesel-mechanical form but with distinctly futuristic styling. Sir WG Armstrong, Whitworth & Co made proposals in 1931 for what was described as an 0-4-4 diesel-electric locomotive with jackshaft drive but this fell on deaf ears, despite contemporary progress in the USA with this form of motive power. The GWR only ever operated one diesel-electric locomotive, an 0-6-0 shunter.

Electricity generated by gas-turbine power was cutting edge technology and its adoption in late 1945 /early 1946 in partnership with Metropolitan-Vickers was a revolutionary project whose genesis is discussed further below. A little later an additional locomotive was ordered from Brown-Boveri in Switzerland. Operationally both suffered through inclusion in existing rosters and maintenance in traditional MPD facilities. Both 18000 and 18100 incurred an undue number of failures several of which were attributed to dirt and grime accumulated in shed conditions. This background was a key factor in the Western Region policy decision to eschew electricity and employ hydraulic transmission in its main line locomotive fleet under the BR Modernisation Plan.

Dick Riley's recording of diesel power seems to have been concurrent with but incidental to his studies of steam. Thus, as steam receded so did his black and white photographic work and while the early diesel-hydraulics of Classes D600, D800, D6300 and Beyer Peacock Hymeks do feature, the Westerns are absent. Nevertheless, his record of non-steam motive power provides an interesting survey of the early stages of a process that would so change the face of the old Great Western.

Towards the close of their careers, some surviving railcars were painted in dark BR green with cream whiskers on the ends below the cabs which did not really suit them. W29W, from which the drive shaft connecting the two axles has been removed, was at Worcester on 19th August 1962, in company with No W30W. *RCR 16741.*

The final four GWR railcars (Nos 35-38) were completed in similar style to Nos 19-33 but as two pairs with driving cabs at one end only. Construction was completed during World War 2 when conventional coach building had virtually ceased, an indication of the potential attached by the GWR to the multiple unit principle. No 37 was destroyed by fire in 1947 and in due course was replaced by No 33 which had been rebuilt as a single driving cab unit to work with No 38. Passenger capacity was increased by insertion of a suitably modified ordinary coach between the driving vehicles. In this view taken on 19th August 1962, railcar Nos 35 and 36 are departing Worcester with a Brake Composite (Diagram E146 or E148) in between. *RCR 16740.*

The solitary diesel-electric locomotive owned by the GWR as at 31st December 1947 was English Electric-built 0-6-0 shunter No 2. It was renumbered by BR as 15100, the only GWR locomotive to be treated in this fashion as a result of nationalisation. In 1946, power units for six similar locomotives were ordered from the same manufacturer with remaining construction undertaken by Swindon works. These locomotives were delivered between April and July 1948 and numbered 15101-6; in outward appearance, they were similar to the standard BR Class 08 shunter. No 15103 was at Old Oak Common on 28th November 1954. *RCR 5647.*

The Gloster Meteor entered service as the Royal Air Force's first operational jet fighter in July 1944. Concern to protect the plane's revolutionary and top secret technology was such that it was forbidden to enter enemy airspace. It was therefore surprising that the GWR, an inherently conservative organisation, should avoid contemporary diesel motive power and opt for the technologically cutting-edge gas turbine engine that derived directly from that used in the Meteor.

Board and management moved fast at the end of 1945 in approving a joint venture with Metropolitan-Vickers for construction of a gas turbine-powered locomotive, which was eventually completed as Co Co BR No 18100 in late 1952. Brown-Boveri of Switzerland was contracted in September 1946 to construct a second locomotive that was delivered in 1950 as A1A+A1A BR 18000.

How and why the construction of 18100 was approved has never been explained but circumstantially, a number of factors could have been relevant:

- Sir William Stanier presumably met Sir Frank Whittle in the early 1930s when both were collaborating with Metropolitan-Vickers concerning turbine design – the former in connection with LMS Turbomotive No 6202, the latter in connection with the Gloster-Whittle, the very first British jet aircraft. Towards the end of the war, Stanier was appointed a director of Whittle's company, Power Jets Ltd.
- Sir Felix Pole, General Manager of the GWR, had left in 1929 to become Chairman of Associated Electrical Industries, the parent company of Metropolitan-Vickers.
- Hawksworth, CME at Swindon 1941-8 was a colleague and personal friend of Stanier.
- Stanier and Sir James Milne (G.M. of the GWR until November 1947) were brothers-in-law.

No 18100 was not a success being shorter-lived than No 18000 with a greater incidence of problems, including defects in bogie design. Intended as an express machine, the technology's potential was nonetheless proven in load tests in November 1952 when it hauled 17 coaches (590 tons) unassisted from Plymouth to Newton Abbot. Here, No 18100 is on less demanding work near Moreton Cutting between Didcot and Cholsey & Moulsford on 4th July 1953.

The engine entered normal service in April 1952, and by withdrawal in December 1953 had covered 75,000 miles but with 25 major failures in the process. It was agreed that Metropolitan-Vickers should modify the power unit to use heavy oil which measure was felt might improve performance. This work proceeded slowly and was eventually abandoned in 1957 when the joint venture was wound up. The engine had a subsequent career as an electrification test locomotive. *RCR 3986.*

CORNISH RIVIERA EXPRESS
D602

D823
D 823
IV98

Opposite top: A legacy of the gas turbine experience was the determination to avoid electric transmission in the modernisation fleet. Reportedly there was disagreement via-á-vis the broader policy objectives of the British Transport Commission so the first express diesel type, North British-built A1A+A1A "Warship" Class D600 was an awkward compromise. Hydraulic transmission was sanctioned but not the then revolutionary idea of stressed-skin lightweight construction. The result was a locomotive with two MAN 12 cylinder high-revving diesel engines within a body of obsolete design. The weight was approximately 118 tons, not significantly less than the English Electric 1Co-Co1 against which it was compared in the Type 4 power category. Only five were built and from 1958 onwards, all were allocated to Laira depot from where they worked principal expresses to and from Paddington until there were sufficient of Warship Class D800 to displace them. Thereafter they operated mainly west of Plymouth. As a numerically small, non-standard class, these engines were early withdrawal candidates and all were taken out of service in December 1967. They had a proven capacity for fast running but gained a reputation for poor reliability, although they may have been no worse than other early diesel types in this respect. Indeed, maintenance staff at Laira considered that their performance was acceptable. D602 *Bulldog* was still on top link work on 8th June 1960 at Westbourne Park, heading the down "Cornish Riviera Express". *RCR 15228.*

Opposite bottom: In pursuit of the diesel-hydraulic principle, Swindon negotiated a licence with German manufacturers to produce a scaled down version of German Federal Railways type V200. The result was B -B Class D800 (later Class 42) which externally and internally closely followed the German machine. Power was provided by a pair of Maybach 1035 hp (Nos D800-2) engines, increased to 1135 hp for Nos D803 onwards. These engines were built by Bristol Siddeley under licence, while the remainder of the construction, following the German design format, was undertaken by Swindon works. These locomotives, also named after warships, were conceptually advanced. Their power output was similar to contemporary Diesel-Electric 1Co-Co1 designs (D1 later Class 44 and D200 Class 40) whose chassis and body design dated back to prototype LMS diesels of the late 1940s. The diesel hydraulics weighed slightly under 80 tons, carried on four axles whereas Class 44 weighed 138 tons and Class 40 133 tons – both carried on eight axles. The lower weight was proven to be advantageous as between London & Birmingham, Swindon's product proved at least a coach stronger than Class 40. Externally, Class 42 was compact with clean, elegant lines. When introduced, their outward appearance was perhaps not appreciated by the steam-orientated enthusiast fraternity but together with the later Western Class, they were arguably the most handsome of British Railways diesel classes. Certainly, D823 *Hermes* makes a pleasing sight at Laira depot on 30th April 1961 and definitely superior to the stubby-bodied examples of North British-built Class D63xx behind. *RCR 15685.*

Below: Although intended initially as express passenger locomotives, the D8xx Warships were soon found on a range of less prestigious duties. On 24th September 1960, No D816 *Eclipse* was at St Blazey yard with a Fowey-bound china clay train. *RCR 16070.*

B-B Warship Class 43 Nos 833 to 865 were externally similar to Class 42 but built by North British Locomotive Co with MAN L12V engines (between 1960 and 1962). These proved less reliable than the Maybach units installed in Class 42 and so they were withdrawn earlier. D834 *Pathfinder* was at Ranelagh Bridge on 13th August 1960 in company with No 4084 *Aberystwyth Castle*. The Castle was withdrawn the following October after a 35-year career; the Class 43 was taken out of service in October 1971 after an 11-year career. *RCR 15272.*

Fifty-eight examples of Class D63xx built by North British Locomotive Co were delivered between 1959 and 1962. They had a single 1000 hp/1100hp MAN L12V power unit with similar control and transmission equipment to that installed in the twin-engine D6xx Warship Class. Externally they looked like a stub-ended version of the earlier North British machines and were inevitably referred to as "Baby Warships". Intended for secondary duties (local passenger and freight work), they were concentrated in the West Country but also with small contingents in the London and Bristol areas. Reliability was an early concern but BR had negotiated a service support agreement with the manufacturers for repairs and modifications. Performance was improved with availability levels reaching about 85% before North British unfortunately went out of business in 1962. This presented BR with a spare parts problem that could only be solved through cannibalisation. Withdrawals commenced in 1967 and the class became extinct in January 1972. D6317 was at Bodmin Road on 13th July 1961 with a 2-coach B-Set bound for Bodmin General. *RCR 16084.*

Above: During the steam/ diesel transition phase, it was common practice for the two technologies to work together over the south Devon banks. Whenever possible, the diesel would act as the lead or pilot engine to prevent smoke and ash entering the air intakes, and the envelopment of its cab in steam exhaust. D6325 is piloting No 7026 *Tenby Castle* at Tavistock Junction on 8th July 1961. If a steam engine was leading, enthusiasts automatically assumed yet another failure... *RCR 16043.*

Below: Curiously, no views of D1000 "Western" Class diesels have been traced in the Riley Collection but there are several of the contemporary diesel-hydraulic Hymeks, built by a joint venture between Beyer Peacock and Bristol Siddeley. There were 101 examples of this class and they were reasonably successful. However, all were all withdrawn between 1971 and 1975 due to their non-standard status and the impending introduction of electrically heated coaching stock. Their range of duties was fairly extensive including reaching places like Ilfracombe where No D7095 was recorded on 2nd July 1964. By then the LSWR's Withered Arm was under BR Western Region control. *RCR 17672.*

This Dean era 4-wheel coach appears to have started life as a First/ Second Composite, later relegated to First/ Third, and finally assigned to Departmental duties. As a composite coach, it would have been included in the U-Diagram series but it has not been possible to identity the suffix. The running number does not help as it duplicates that of a Diagram K40 Passenger Brake Van built November 1931. *RCR 3147.*

The GWR generally preferred first class accommodation to be provided in composite vehicles which meant that All First coaches were comparatively scarce. At nationalisation, there were ten clerestory All Firsts still at work in the following diagrams:- A4 non-corridor [one coach]; A7 [seven]; A8 [two]. This undated view, believed to be at Aberystwyth, shows Diagram A7 No W8135W, built November 1902 and withdrawn May 1952. This 58' coach had a corridor section that gave access to five compartments and a 2-bay open saloon (left of picture). Two toilets were provided on the far side, one between the saloon and the compartment section, and the other at the coach end on the right. Metal sheeting has been applied to some of the panelled bodywork below the waist but this late survivor is in remarkably original condition.

Following withdrawal from general service, it was converted to Camping Coach No W9900W and served in this role until December 1963. *RCR 3279.*

Chapter 4

Coaches

At the end of 1938, the GWR mustered a fleet of 6,168 passenger-carrying vehicles with an average age of 18 years. Other than to fulfil outstanding orders, new coach building all but ceased during the war years. When construction resumed in earnest in 1946, the fleet total was down to 5,738 as a result of war damage and withdrawals based on age or condition. Coaches awaiting repair or overdue servicing had risen from 6% to 22% of the fleet total, and even after 12 months of peace, the company was still providing 250 passenger trains a week to meet governmental and military demands.

New construction did little to redress the situation. Plans prepared in 1944 anticipated five new coaches a week i.e. 260 in the year 1946 but acute shortages of materials and personnel meant that only 518 of the Hawksworth 64' mainline coaches were produced in seven years. There was a similar need for suburban stock but the construction programme for Hawksworth's spacious 63' coaches did not start until 1948 and by 1953 had produced only 441 vehicles.

Coaches were the shop front so far as the travelling public was concerned and tired, outmoded and inadequately maintained vehicles did little for the railway's image and reputation. The situation was unavoidable given the conditions under which services were maintained during hostilities and in the immediately succeeding years. So far as the enthusiast was concerned, service retention of many otherwise time-expired vehicles during the GWR's closing years and well into nationalisation was a bonus. While Dick Riley did not focus specifically on studies of coaches, he did capture enough to show how interesting train composition could be in those years.

Another Dean era survivor was All Third No 3113, a 46' 6" Diagram C10 non-corridor, 8-compartment, 80-seat clerestory coach of which over 100 examples entered the BR fleet. This coach, which was at Rhymney on 10th May 1952, was built in February 1898 and stayed in service until August 1953.

To the right can be seen the end of another veteran, in this case ex-Taff Vale Railway Third No W2528W (originally TVR No 365). This non-corridor coach was 60' 10" long and accommodated 100 passengers in 10 compartments. ***RCR 3469.***

Above: Newcastle Emlyn was one of the more remote outposts of the Great Western system. It was at the end of the 10-mile branch line from Pencader Junction on the winding route from Carmarthen to Aberystwyth. This was a natural habitat for 0-4-2T Class 14xx No 1472 as seen here running round at the terminus on 30th July 1951. The train comprises a single toplight slip coach whose number cannot be seen. Confirmation of the diagram is prevented by the open doors which block the view of the windows and their relative spacing. However, it is most probably a 57' Diagram F16 Double Slip with guard and luggage accommodation nearest the camera, corridor on this side giving access to four third class compartments, then a toilet, followed by two first class compartments, and finally a guard's compartment at the far end. Ten of this type were built 1909-10 and the nine survivors were designated Non-Corridor Brake Composite in March 1954. It would seem that this vehicle had been dedicated to branch work in advance of this reclassification. *RCR 3205.*

Opposite top: In addition to revolutionary locomotive development, Churchward fostered a new generation of passenger coaches that was influenced by contemporary practice in the USA. Changing construction methods meant greater use of steel that resulted in increased tare weight per passenger. Seventy feet long coaches were a means of counteracting this trend. By this yardstick, the 54' Dean Clerestory Second/ Third Class coach was possibly the company's most efficient design in accommodating 2.67 passengers for every tare ton. By comparison, the ratio for a 70' steel panelled coach of 1914 vintage was 2.25 (and for a 63' British Railways Mark 1 it was 1.73).

The 70' by 9' 6" Dreadnought coaches first appeared in the form of restaurant cars in 1904 with first and third class coaches arriving the following year. These vehicles exploited the generous GWR loading gauge to the full and were revolutionary in their massive size, and in their having only six external doors (at either end and in the middle) which were recessed into the body sides. The travelling public, accustomed to doors to each compartment on both sides, objected to access only by means of the corridor, making these imposing coaches unpopular.

As a compromise, the next design combined the Dreadnoughts' outside dimensions with external access to each compartment by means of recessed doors. The result gave rise to the nickname by which these coaches were known – Concertina. Slip coach Diagram F13 No W7695 was at Carmarthen on 9th May 1951 in company with what appeared to be another slip coach to the right and a non-corridor suburban vehicle to the left.

This coach was built in August 1906 as a 70' Tri-composite Slip (from left to right – guard and luggage accommodation/ toilet/ three x third class compartments/ two x first class compartments/ two x second class compartments/ toilet/ guard and luggage accommodation). The second class accommodation was later down-graded to third class. It would seem that by 1951 this vehicle was no longer engaged on slip duties. No W7695 was withdrawn in July 1953 and the following year the five of this type still in service were formally reclassified as Non-Corridor Brake Composites. *RCR 3944.*

This page, bottom: Following on from the Concertina era, the GWR continued with the 70' theme in the Toplight coach series of which Diagram E93 Composite No W7762 was an example. Built in April 1914, there was seating for 24 first class passengers in four compartments and for 40 third class passengers in five compartments, with a toilet at either end. Looking rather tired in this undated photograph and now condemned, this handsome vehicle is probably standing at Swindon having been withdrawn in May 1956. Over a long working career the body panelling has not stood up too well to the elements necessitating the fitting of steel plate over some sections. *RCR Ref unconfirmed.*

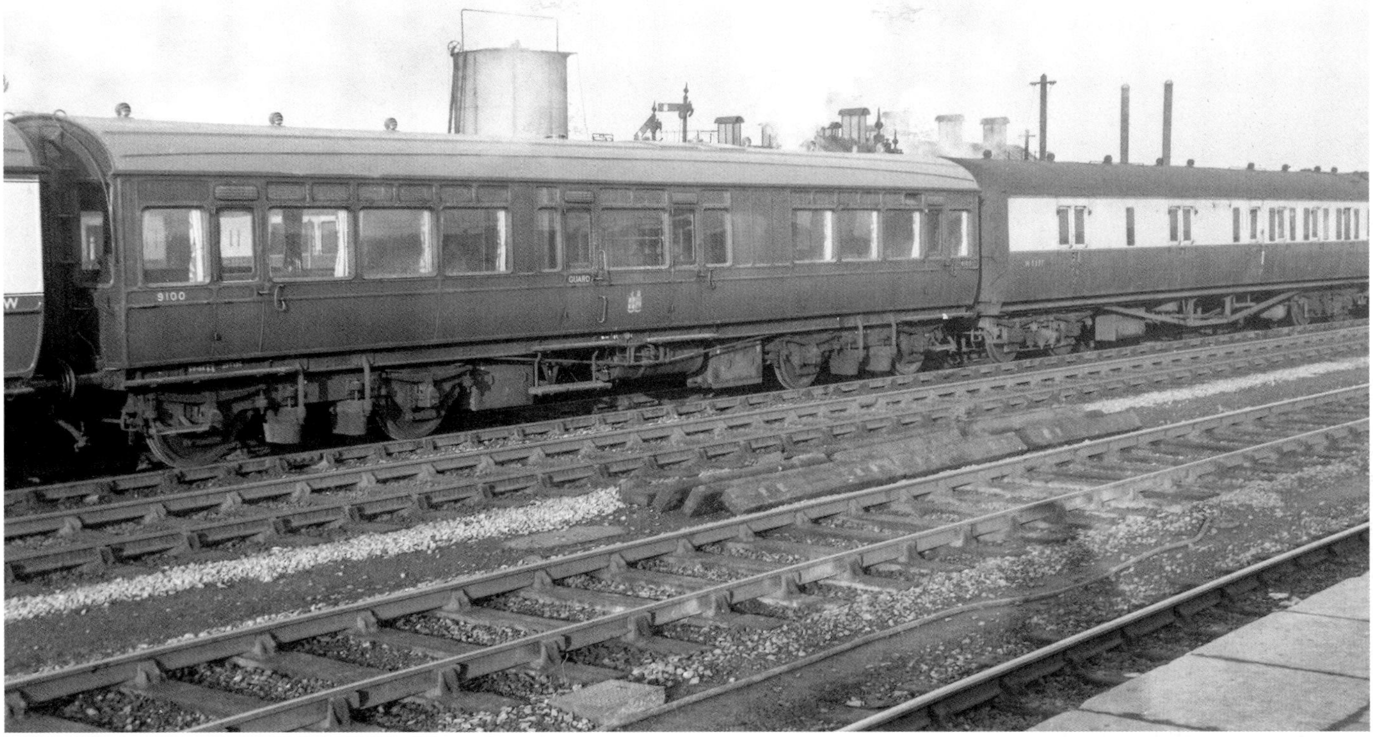

This page: Coach No 9100 was a unique toplight vehicle dating from August 1912, originally a Diagram Q Inspection Saloon that was later reclassified as a Diagram G57 Nondescript Saloon. Its 54' 0" long body was divided into three sections of equal length. There were saloons at either end connected by a side corridor through the central section, the rest of which contained sleeping accommodation, kitchen and toilet. It remained in service until September 1954 when it was converted to office accommodation.

The saloon was coupled to 61' 4" Diagram D111 bow-ended Brake Third No 5377 (built March 1931, withdrawn September 1961) when passing Swindon on 12th January 1953. *RCR 3846.*

Opposite top: The Toplight style was also applied to suburban stock as with Diagram E103 non-corridor Composite No 7924 built in February 1922 and withdrawn October 1958. The place is Caerphilly yard on 11th May 1952 and on the left is part of the van end of a 57' Collett-era non-corridor Brake Third of Diagram D85. In the right background is a corridor Toplight that appears to have been refurbished and modernised, but is too distant for confirmation of its identity. *RCR 3481.*

Opposite bottom: The GWR maintained a small fleet of saloon coaches whose accommodation took a variety of layouts. They were usually confined to special duties but did occasionally turn up in normal service trains at busy periods (particularly Collett-era Diagrams G56 and G58). No 9365 was one of three that had started life in 1901 as ambulance coaches being later re-designated Diagram G54. The compact 46' 6" by 8' 6" body was divided into two open saloons of equal size that together accounted for about 80% of the internal body length with two toilets at both ends. External access was by a single side door on either side to each saloon.

After ambulance duties, No 9365 became a Third Saloon equipped with longitudinal seats along the sides, and with longitudinal tables in between. It was taken out of running service in March 1951 and converted to office accommodation being renumbered DW302 in March 1954 and later 079016. In this view, it was standing in Llandovery shed on 8th September 1951. *RCR 3415.*

Taff Vale Railway non-corridor Third No 335 built in 1902 was 49' 3" long and accommodated 80 passengers. It became GWR No 2491 and was one of 18 that survived long enough to enter the BR fleet. It was at Rhymney on 10th May 1952, and remained in service until March 1954. ***RCR 3467.***

Barry Railway non-corridor No 151 was built as a 52' 6" Tri-composite vehicle. By the time it passed into British Railways ownership, it had become First/ Third Composite No 6126 with seating for 24 First and 50 Third Class passengers. It was at Caerphilly on 11th May 1952 and continued in service until April 1959. ***RCR 3479.***

This photograph exemplifies the problem of categorising some of Dick Riley's work as this view could equally qualify for inclusion in the chapters on Trains or Locomotives. The date is 4th July 1959 and Castle Class No 7037 *Swindon* is piloting Class 68xx No 6830 *Buckenhill Grange* on an Up express near Bath Spa.

However, it is the first coach that is the main source of interest as it appears to be a catering vehicle working in ordinary passenger service. The distance is too great to discern the running number but process of deduction suggests that by virtue of the flush (i.e. non-recessed) doors and the 6-wheel bogies, this is either a Diagram H50 First Diner or a Diagram H51 Third Diner. When the GWR introduced articulated 8-coach main line sets in 1925, catering was provided by an articulated trio comprising Restaurant First (48 seats) + Kitchen Car + Restaurant Third (64 seats). These facilities were soon found to be over-generous and one or two conventional catering vehicles were substituted. The other articulated groups (Brake First + All First and All Third + All Third + Brake Third) were divided and given conventional bogies in 1936/ 7. The catering trios were similarly treated a little later. In both articulated and conventional form, the Restaurant Cars (later termed Diners) were internally and externally identical except for 3-aside or 4-aside seating bays. On conversion, two of each diagram received 6-wheel bogies. Why this was done is unclear because internally they comprised a single saloon without even toilet facilities and were thus in weight equal to or lighter than contemporary ordinary coaches. Examples of both diagrams survived until 1962.

The following coach appears to be a Collett-era bow-ended Brake Composite. *RCR 13718.*

Above: On 23rd July 1951, 0-6-0PT Class 74xx No 7440 was engaged in what appears to be a shunting movement at Bala Junction on the GWR's route from Ruabon/ Wrexham that in pre-Grouping days made a head-on connection with the Cambrian Railway at Dolgelly. At the junction, a line branched away in a north-westward direction through Bala and Trawsfynydd, and then wound its way northward through Festiniog to terminate at Blaenau Festiniog Central.

The coach is No W7965W, the first of a batch of twenty-five flat-ended 57' Brake Composites introduced in July 1923 to Diagram E114. This was a useful vehicle type that embraced all the essential features of a mainline passenger train, except for catering facilities. Accommodation consisted of two first class compartments seating 12, five third class compartments seating 32, two toilets, and a guard/ luggage section. Brake Composites were regularly used on single coach through workings over other companies' routes and to this end No 7965 was one of nine whose equipment included Westinghouse brake for operating compatibility where that system was in use. It was withdrawn in June 1957. *RCR Ref unconfirmed.*

Opposite top: Hawksworth Class 15xx 0-6-0PT No 1505 was engaged in carriage shunting at Old Oak Common on either 4th February or 20th May 1956. The coaches are a pair of Super Saloons, that in front being Diagram H45 All First with seating for 24 passengers, plus a kitchen and one toilet, built in May 1932. When introduced (and later in preservation after withdrawal in August 1966), this coach was named *Princess Elizabeth*. The identity of the saloon behind is not clear. These coaches led privileged existences and were usually stored under cover at OOC. *RCR Ref unconfirmed.*

Opposite bottom: Great Western mainline trains often displayed a variety of styles and profiles, as is apparent in this view of a County-hauled Truro-bound service. The leading vehicle is No W6421W, a 60' 11" Brake Composite of Diagram E159 dating from February 1938 whereas the Composite following cannot be specifically identified but is of pre-1933 vintage. Differences are obvious in the body profiles, the heights of the cant rail and waist, the depths of the windows, and the pronounced tumblehome of the second coach compared with the sheer side and lower taper of the other.
RCR Ref unconfirmed.

1505

TRURO

After their normal careers had ended, some veterans found further income-earning work in the form of camping coaches as with No W9906W at Luxulyan between Par and Bugleon on 18th July 1960. This coach had commenced life in May 1902 as No 1472, the prototype of 55' First/ Second corridor Composite Diagram E73. It was later reclassified as First/ Third Composite and renumbered 4472. Its accommodation was then 18 first class passengers in three compartments and 32 third class passengers in eight compartments with a toilet at either end. After a service career of exactly 50 years, it was converted to a Camping Coach and finally withdrawn in April 1965. *RCR 15111.*

Chapter 5
Locations

Of all the pre-Grouping railways, the Great Western was the largest by route mileage. Rather than focus on the major stations, junctions etc, this chapter partly seeks to provide a flavour of what could be found in the less well-known corners of the Western Region.

Above: Pannier tank yard pilots or shunters almost invariably went about their humble yet essential duties accompanied by a shunter's truck (or gig). These handy little riding vehicles must have been greatly appreciated by those engaged in the physically arduous work of coupling/ uncoupling wagons. They had a close affinity with their home base whose name would appear on the tool box, as with Westbury's No DW 94995 seen here on 13th July 1964. Many gigs worked long lives in the same area and when repair was no longer justifiable thus necessitating total replacement, the new version would return "home" with its place of work in evidence and often carrying its predecessor's running number. *RCR 17647.*

Right: Gerrards Cross viewed from the footplate on a down train. The date is 23rd April 1960 and the locomotive is No 6003 *King George IV.* At this time traffic was concentrated on the GWR's Paddington-Birmingham route while electrification of the ex-LMS line was in hand, thereby giving the Kings an extra lease of life. *RCR 14675.*

Above: Newbury races offered a pleasant day out and many from London availed themselves of the opportunity, including directors and senior officers of the GWR, judging by the railway facilities provided. On 5th March 1960, special trains were standing at Newbury Racecourse, to the south of the mainline and half-a-mile east of the main station. Castle Class No 5074 *Hampden* is to the left with No 6010 *King Charles I* alongside. *RCR 14718.*

Above: No 6010 has now moved forward to be turned on the table in front of Newbury Racecourse Signal Box. *RCR 14517.*

Below: The railway also took care of the horses. Churchward 2-6-0 No 6313 is shunting horseboxes at Newbury Racecourse on 5th March 1960. *RCR 14520.*

A London-bound unidentified Hall approaches the ornate west end of St. Anne's Park (No 2) Tunnel, Bristol on 19th September 1955. (St. Anne's No 1 Tunnel which had been about a quarter of a mile to the west was opened out in 1889). Despite the date, the Coats of Arms of London and Bristol are still in evidence on the Hall's tender, the relevant area having been specially cleaned. The leading coach is No W5354W, a 61' 4" bow-ended Collett All Third (Diagram C60) built in June 1930 and withdrawn in March 1962. *RCR Ref unconfirmed.*

Another ornate tunnel-related feature was this ventilator for the 4440-yard Chipping Sodbury Tunnel to the west of Badminton, photographed on 18th September 1955. Construction in this style was at the insistence of the Duke of Beaufort who felt that it would be pleasing to the eye when viewed from his estate. ***RCR 6796.***

Below: Protect the dreaming spires. Lest there be any doubt about this location, the sign just beyond the platform ramp advises "*The emission of smoke from engines must be reduced to the absolute minimum in the Oxford area*". Castle Class No 5075 *Wellington* awaits the "right away" on 21st April 1956 as War Department 2-8-0 No 90313 trundles southwards on an unfitted freight. Major GWR stations were always enhanced by a profusion of fine signals and Oxford was no exception. ***RCR 7136.***

Right: On 15th July 1961, Dick Riley captured this quaint link with the past on a gable end at Newton Abbot shed. It should not be confused with the rather more ornate vane that decorated the nearby works building. *RCR 16117.*

Below: Oxford's splendid array of signals is shown from another angle as Castle Class No 7005 *Sir Edward Elgar* arrived on 15th August 1959 with an express, appropriately enough, from Worcester. Built in June 1946, this locomotive had been *Lamphey Castle* until August 1957, being the last of the class to undergo a change of identity. *RCR 14083.*

On 12th July 1955, Hawksworth-designed 0-6-0PT Class 94xx No 8425 was shunting at Plymouth Millbay Docks. Behind the fixed distant signal, the notice on the wall states:

GREAT WESTERN RAILWAY
COMPANY'S SERVANTS ONLY ALLOWED TO
WALK TO AND FROM THE DOCKS THROUGH
THIS MILEAGE YARD.
TRESPASSERS WILL BE PROSECUTED
BY ORDER

Just visible to the extreme left is a Morris Minor Tourer– probably Dick Riley's trusty steed. ***RCR 6417.***

Class 1361 0-6-0ST No 1364 was working at the same place on 12th July 1955, in this case accompanied by a shunter's truck labelled "Plymouth Docks". ***RCR 6418.***

Bodmin Road Station was awkwardly sited on the West of England mainline and an unusual supply system was necessary to feed the crane on the up platform. On 12th July 1956, small Prairie No 4565 was taking water while standing on the line to Bodmin General. "Road" in a station title usually indicated that the settlement to which it referred was not in the immediate vicinity. In this case, a journey of around four miles along the branch brought the passenger to "General" and thus, Cornwall's county town. *RCR 7604.*

Quieter corners:

Dick Riley kept an eye on minor stations that would not normally receive much attention but which had features so redolent of the old GWR:

Right: Shipston-on-Stour. This was the terminus of the freight only branch from Moreton-in-Marsh on the Oxford-Worcester route. The date was 24th April 1955 and the occasion was an enthusiasts' special that was worked by 0-6-0 Dean Goods No 2474. *RCR 6080.*

Bottom: Probus & Ladock Platform. Looking west on the Cornish main line between Grampound Road and Truro on 7th July 1955, this modest stopping place is a typical GWR halt – timber platforms, gas lighting, pagoda corrugated waiting shelters, and board crossing. *RCR 6307.*

Left: Savernake Low Level. Located between Newbury and Westbury on the Berks & Hants line on 8th July 1956, looking west with the Marlborough branch forking way to the right. ***RCR 7483.***

Bottom: Savernake High Level. This was on the old Midland & South Western line, and set a little to the north of the GWR’s Low Level station. By 8th July 1956, this route’s secondary status was apparent in the right-hand road being reduced to provision of storage for vans and Toads. Dick Riley’s Morris is parked beside the station entrance. ***RCR 7484.***

Collingbourne Kingston Halt. Visited on 8th July 1956, this ex-M&SWJR halt between Ludgershall and Savernake High Level does not have quite the style of the GWR establishment at Probus & Ladock Platform. There is electric lighting but only in its most basic form, and the corrugated waiting shelters are little more than garden sheds. There is no board crossing; the sign at the end of the left-hand platform enjoined passengers to cross the line by way of the road bridge. *RCR 7479.*

Ogbourne. The first station after Marlborough travelling northwards on the M&SWJR, visited on 14th May 1955. *RCR 6104.*

1M99

This page: Trains for the Blenheim & Woodstock Branch parted company with the Oxford-Aynho/ Banbury route at Kidlington and ran parallel with the main line for about a mile before turning away in a westerly direction. Slightly less than two miles before the terminus stood the branch's only intermediate stopping place, Shipton-on-Chirwell Halt. The date is 27th February 1954 and as regards nationalisation, the signage suggests that this rural outpost had yet to join the scheme. *RCR 5022.*

Opposite top: Bovey. This was the station for the small town of Bovey Tracey on the Newton Abbot - Moretonhampstead Branch, portrayed on 17th July 1958. This picturesque line closed to passengers on 28th February the following year, and to all traffic on 9th April 1964. The writing must have been on the wall at the time of Dick Riley's visit yet the station and its grounds are still beautifully tended. *RCR 12326.*

Opposite bottom: End of the line and all change! – well not quite yet on 24th September 1960 at Penzance. Modernity is present in the form of B-B Warship Class 42 No D820 *Grenville* but much of the old order remains. In the short stub siding there are a pair of Cordon travelling gas tank wagons. A 2-tank Diagram DD5 stands closer to the camera while a familiar 9-tank Diagram DD4 version is behind. Alongside is a Collett Brake composite of 1936-8 vintage – Diagram E152, E153 or E155. Platform lighting is gas – hence the Cordons – and on the far line there is an inside-framed Siphon G coupled to what appears to be an ex-LMS passenger brake. The rather grim train shed forms the backdrop. *RCR 15405.*

MULE
INCHCAPE

BRITISH RAILWAYS
BRENTFORD DOCK

Opposite page: At Southall, the focus was on the mainline with little attention paid to the branch that trailed in on the down side behind the locomotive depot. This was, by way of Trumpers Crossing Halt, the 3.3-mile line to Brentford with the Docks a few hundred yards beyond. With his eye for the more obscure, Dick Riley recorded details of this short branch line and this is a vignette of his studies. *Top left*: 0-6-0PT No 8750 with gig at Brentford Docks yard on 8th March 1958. *Top right*: Brentford Docks. *Bottom left*: New ownership emblazoned upon the safety equipment, but.... *Bottom right*: ... not so with the Brentford Dock station building. *RCR 11466 / 11468 / 11467 / 11469.*

Bottom: This chapter commenced with a shunter's truck that clearly displayed its sense of place, and so ends with a Toad brake van also plainly branded with where it belongs. Toads were usually labelled with the name of their home yard or depot and sometimes, as in the case of this 20-ton example, with the route to which they were dedicated. W68776 seen here on 27th February 1954 was confined to use between Kidlington and Blenheim & Woodstock, a route distance of around five miles.

Further limitations are evident from the additional branding, although of little practical significance in this case. "R.U." meant restricted use i.e. confinement within the Western Region's boundaries as brake vehicles should be fitted with side lookout duckets, a ruling from which Toads were excluded. "Not in Common Use" was a broadly similar injunction to the effect that this vehicle was not in the wagon pool that had been started during World War 1 and which by nationalisation had all lines application, except for special cases.

The wagon to the right formed part of the largest single expansion of the pool when on 3rd September 1939 the government requisitioned between 600,000 and 700,000 previously used/ owned by collieries, industrial companies and merchants. This was a wartime measure to improve fleet utilisation in the movement of minerals and freight which hitherto had been grossly inefficient. Following requisition, the number 80048 (the P-prefix is not visible) was issued to North West Wagon Co Ltd of Wednesbury, which had either rented out or had maintained the vehicle for the private operator whose identity is only partially visible on the side. *RCR 5082.*

Studies of Ranelagh Bridge Engine Sidings:-

Top: A panoramic view of the sidings on 30th March 1957 with four locomotives waiting to reverse into the terminus to start their next duties. From left to right: (i) A Britannia carrying the "Capitals United" headboard. (ii) A Castle with a coat of arms on the splasher face making it probably No 7007 *Great Western*. (iii) No 1009 *County of Carmarthen.* (iv) No 6006 *King George I.* The site was certainly snug with the turntable tucked neatly behind Westbourne Bridge Signal Box. *RCR 10373.*

Middle: Another busy period on 27th August 1960, following revision of the reporting number system on an alpha-numeric basis, as introduced with the 1959 winter timetable. From left to right: (i) A County has reversed into the sidings from Paddington and is taking water prior to moving onto the table for turning. (ii) A BR Britannia, possibly No 70025 *Western Star*. (iii) A double chimney Castle, apparently in the 7000-number series, bearing reporting number J39 (12.45 pm Mon-Sat Paddington-Hereford). (iv) Another double chimney Castle coupled to a Hawksworth tender. (v) Single chimney Castle, No 5044 *Earl of Dunraven* with reporting number No F46 (1.55 pm Mon-Sat Paddington-Neyland) (vi) Double chimney King, possibly No *6011 King James I*, carrying reporting number No A16 (7.30 am Mon-Sat Shrewsbury-Paddington). *RCR 15316.*

Chapter 6

Motive power depots

The distance between the buffer stops at Paddington and Old Oak Common East Signal Box located at the entrance to the OOC yards was a crowded 2.6 miles. It therefore made operational sense to minimise light engine and conflicting movements over that stretch. Ranelagh Bridge Engine Sidings, not really a depot in the accepted sense, played an important role in turning and servicing express locomotives between arrival and departure on their next turn of duty. Judging by the number of photographs in his Collection, Dick Riley was a habitual visitor at Ranelagh Bridge. He was possibly aided by a laisse faire attitude towards unofficial visitors who acted maturely.

Visits embraced depots well beyond the immediate London area, as later images show.

Left: On 12th March 1959, No 70019 *Lightning* was having the "Capitals United" headboard affixed prior to being turned while a Castle waits in line. *RCR 11480.*

This page: Chester-allocated 4-6-0 County Class No 1022 *County of Northampton* awaits it next turn on 18th May 1956. Another 4-6-0 stands to the right while the trains in the background reflect the typically busy nature of this location. *RCR 7226.*

Further out at Old Oak Common Roundhouse:-

On 11th April 1964, Old Oak Common could still provide scenes reminiscent of past glories. From left to right, the identities of this group and their withdrawal dates: (i) No 4080 *Powderham Castle* [August 1964]. (ii) No 6937 *Conyngham Hall* [December 1965]. (iii) No 6847 *Tidmarsh Hall* [December 1965]. (iv) 2-8-0 Class 47xx No 4703 [May 1964]. *RCR 17486.*

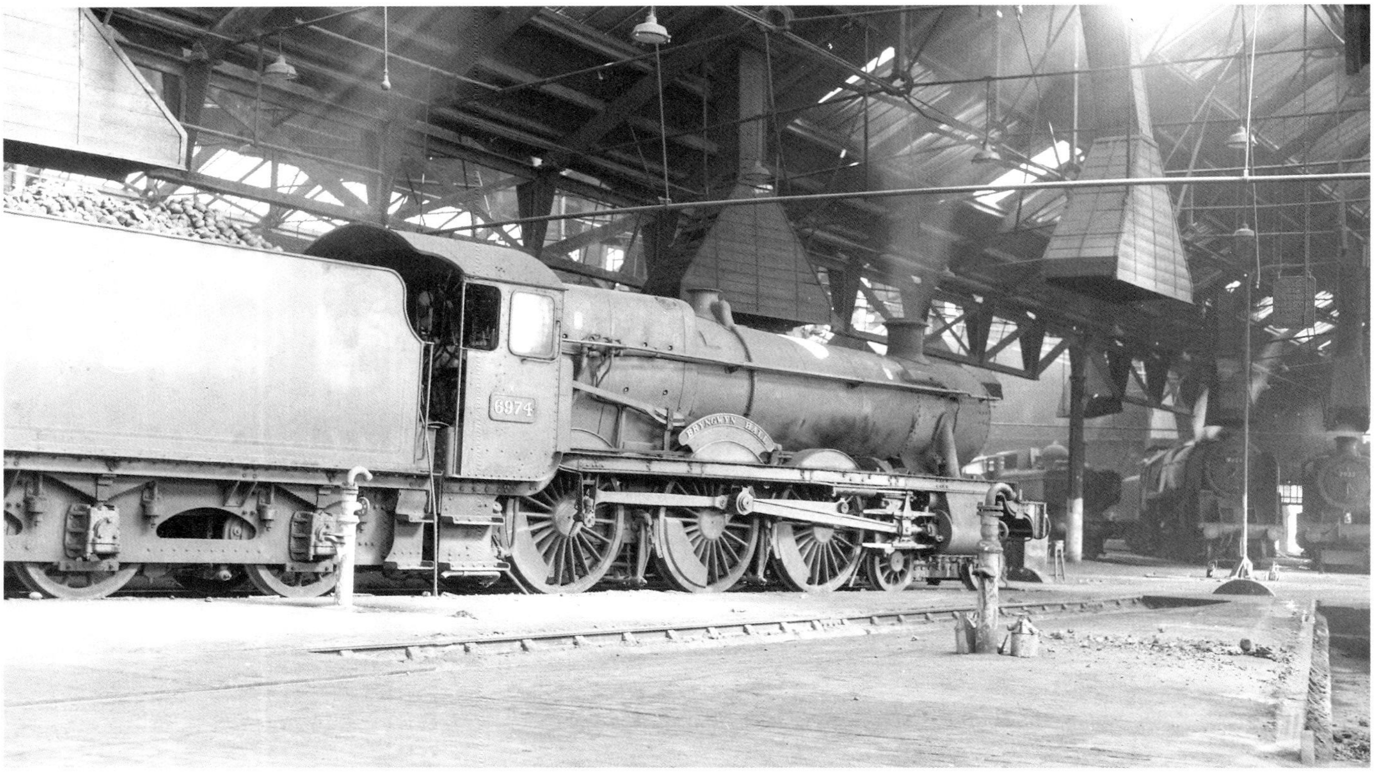

Yet closer to the end of an era, OOC can still muster a few locomotives. On 12th September 1964, reading from left to right: (i) Modified Hall No 6974 *Bryngwyn Hall.* (ii) A Class 8750 pannier tank. (iii) A BR Class 9F 2-10-0. (iv) Modified Hall No 7922 *Salford Hall. RCR 17718*

And beyond…

It is 28th August 1957 and Class 28xx No 2816 stands on the turntable in Swindon round house with 2-6-2T Class 5101 No 5156, 2-6-0 Class 43xx No 6325 and 2-6-2T Class 61xx No 6118 to the left, and an unidentified Hall to the right. *RCR 11150.*

Bottom: In marked contrast to Old Oak Common, Evesham was a sub-shed to Worcester (85A in BR days) on the route from Honeybourne to Worcester. In size and design typical of many rural motive power depots, it backed on to the River Avon and was in the "V" between the GWR and the LMS line on the left which branched away southwards to Ashchurch. On 29th April 1956, there appeared to be a locomotive in the rear of the shed while outside stood (left to right) 94xx 0-6-0PT No 9479, an unidentified 57xx 0-6-0PT and a 2251 0-6-0.
RCR 7186.

Top: No 6848 *Toddington Grange* was at Newton Abbot, its home shed, on 29th August 1954 with an 0-4-2T Class 14xx standing behind. No 5024 *Carew Castle* i shadow to the left and 2-6-2T Class 45xx No 4547 is to the right. *RCR 5311.*

Bottom: 0-6-0ST Class 1361 No 1363 is on the coal stage ramp at Laira Depot or 30th April 1961. This class, which had its design origins in a Cornwall Minerals Railway type, enjoyed a long association with the Plymouth area. No 1363 was t last steam resident of Laira. *RCR 15682.*

Top: St Blazey (SBZ later 83E) motive power depot was a distinctive structure built on the open roundhouse principle much favoured in the USA. The three central roads were about 120’ long and these were flanked on either side by three 70’ roads. The depot was engaged in china clay traffic plus local branch services. Its surprisingly diverse allocation as at 31st December 1947 comprised:- Hall 4-6-0 [2]; 43xx 2-6-0 [2]; 42xx 2-8-0T [2]; 45xx 2-6-2T [7]; 4575 2-6-2T [2]; 5101 2-6-2T [2] plus a varied assembly of 0-6-0 pannier tank classes ancient and modern: 850 [1]; 1854 [1]; 2021 [1]; 2181 [2]; 2780 [1]; 64xx [1]; 57xx [3]; 8750 [1]. There were also pairs of 2-6-2Ts sub-shedded at Bodmin and Moorswater (a 45xx and a 4575 at each). SBZ was a favourite of Dick Riley who visited this far west location at least in September 1954, July 1955, July & September 1960, and July 1961. *RCR 15144.*

Bottom: 1960 is regarded as the last year of plentiful steam in Devon and Cornwall which makes this panoramic view dated 29th April 1961 of Penzance Shed at Long Rock even more pleasing. On show reading from left to right are: Nos 1008 *County of Cardigan*, 6824 *Ashley Grange*, 4920 *Dumbleton Hall*, plus an unidentified Grange and an unidentified Modified Hall. A D8xx Warship lurks in the background. *RCR 15654.*

Top: Smart No 7916 *Mobberley Hall* was being turned at Penzance shed on 29th April 1961. *RCR 15649.*

Left: Subway Junction Signal Box, one of five situated in less than half a mile from Paddington, worked to Westbourne Bridge in the east and to Portobello Junction in the west. Modernisation had arrived in the 1930s with short move pull-push levers operating signals and points although these were still individually controlled, there being no 'route-setting'. The vertical lights on the panel immediately facing the signalman indicated the position/ display of the point/ signal, thus confirming that the required movement had occurred 'on the ground'. Mechanical interlocking existed within the frame as well as electrical locks and track-curcuiting. This view was dated 10th September 1960; the identity of the signalman on duty is unfortunately not known. *RCR 15349.*

Chapter 7

Signal boxes

There are many features, once perceived as permanent fixtures in the railway landscape, that have been eradicated through modernisation. Among the most missed is the traditional signal box that stood as a visible, localised commitment to efficiency and safety that is now exercised through electronic wizardry from distant control centres.

Although certain architectural features were standardised (eg window frames), signal boxes came in a variety of shapes and sizes. There was a correlation between size and traffic volumes. Large boxes inspired awe in the complexity and intensity of their activities whereas at the other end of the scale, small rural boxes generated a particular affection. Without ever ignoring his responsibilities, the Officer would often welcome a chat through the window or even invite the enthusiast into his hallowed domain. Unlike his brethren in the large boxes, his was a solitary existence and he would welcome the company, in between dealing with the bell codes.

Dick Riley obviously liked signal boxes which feature regularly in the Collection. Choosing images for this chapter was complicated in some cases where the locomotive, the train or the location vies for prime attention. Hopefully what follows will provide a nostalgic insight into a near extinct component of the railway.

Southcote Junction Signal Box stood at the point where the Basingstoke branch diverged to the left from the West of England main line. About a quarter mile north of the box, the freight only Coley branch also diverged to the left, and followed a generally U-shaped course over approximately two miles to approach Reading Central Goods Depot, adjacent to the Kennet & Avon Canal, from the south. The Basingstoke branch plus the route to Newbury and beyond were collectively known as the Berks & Hants line. On the extreme left of the picture, the board that is "off" confirms that 0-6-0PT No 5763 was in charge of a local service to Newbury on 20th April 1956, despite carrying a light engine head code. The GWR, and its successor, seemed to delight in using a mixture of stock for secondary services. This rake comprises a suburban non-corridor Brake Third (Diagram D132) of 1948-1953 vintage, followed by two gangwayed vehicles – an All Third (Diagram C54) first introduced in 1925 and then a Brake Composite of Diagram E146 or E148, introduced from 1933 onwards. In the siding to the left stands an iron-bodied workshop or tool van. ***RCR 7123.***

508

Opposite top: Firestone Signal Box on the Brentford Branch was about three miles from Southall and opposite a major rubber factory, hence the name. This view dated 8th March 1958 shows that a box with the normal brick base would have required considerable foundation works so the solution was an all wooden structure supported by timber piers driven into the ground. *RCR 11463.*

Opposite bottom: **Brewham Signal Box was a typical rural affair, of which there were once so many, on the Berks & Hants line between Strap Lane Halt and Witham. No 6998 *Burton Agnes Hall* (phonetically-speaking known to some as "Mr & Mrs Hall") was passing on 2nd July 1955 with the 9.10 am Saturdays only Minehead-Paddington.** *RCR 6163.*

Above: Bristol East Depot Mainline Signal Box was also located on an awkward site being set in a deep cutting between Temple Meads and St Annes stations on the main line to Paddington. The box was placed in an elevated position well above track level, supported by RSJ-type steel beams. The sunlight on 19th September 1955 revealed the exposed nature of the lever rodding which was normally neatly hidden away in the basement. *RCR 6830.*

4136

128
BURLESCOMBE SIGNAL BOX
CATCH POINTS
1156 Yds

Opposite top: Whiteball Siding Signal Box in size was typical of many mainline break-section boxes whose signals were usually left "off" and only switched in by the controlling box at busy periods. This box differed in being permanently manned to control the reversal of locomotives that had assisted trains up Wellington Bank and through Whiteball Tunnel on the Somerset/ Devon border. Class 5101 No 4136 had no need of banking assistance working this Taunton-Exeter local service on 4th September 1954. Once again, the train consist is an interesting variety. Judging by the inset guard's door and the number of compartments, the leading Brake Third might be from Diagram D116, followed by Hawksworth coach, a Sunshine coach, with a Hawksworth Brake Third bringing up the rear. ***RCR 5447.***

Opposite bottom: Burlescombe Signal Box clearly displays its identity as was standard GWR practice and also provides warning of catch points, in this case relating to the industrial line that trailed in from left of picture. This line served Westleigh Quarry from which genuine broad gauge trackwork was recovered some years ago. Through the graceful overbridge can be seen the Up platform of Burlescombe station with Castle Class No 5087 *Tintern Abbey* heading the 10.20 am Saturdays only Paddington-Kingswear on 4th September 1954. ***RCR 5435.***

Above: Exeter Middle Signal Box stood sentinel at the Up end of St Davids station (Down for Southern trains). In partnership with Exeter's east and west boxes, it ensured that correct priorities were maintained over the other company' services from St Davids to Cowley Bridge Junction where the ex-LSWR "Withered Arm" branched away northwards. Bankers were needed to help Southern trains up the 1 in 37 gradient to Exeter Central and they would wait for their next trip on a short stub of a siding below Middle Signal Box. For long, these duties were entrusted to members of 0-6-2T Class E1/R which had been rebuilt in 1927-9 from London Brighton & South Coast Railway 0-6-0T Class E, However, in the closing years of steam, larger tank locomotives declared redundant in the London area took over. Maunsell's 0-8-0T Class Z were used and also his 3-cylinder 2-6-4T Class W, as shown here with Nos 31911/ 2. Following the unhappy history of the River Class 2-6-4Ts, Class W was explicitly (and perhaps quite unnecessarily) restricted to freight duties so presumably this was the closest these competent engines ever came to passenger work. The tarmac in the foreground was part of the level crossing, officially known as Red Cow Crossing, that takes Station Road across the railway. This road then bridges the River Exe to reach the suburb of Exwick. There are too many lines for installation of full gates so there is always a railway employee on duty as a flagman to keep an eye on road traffic during the interludes that no trains are expected. On summer Saturdays, especially in the 1950s and 1960s, road users had to resign themselves to very long waits – but of course they had plenty to watch! ***RCR 17250.***

Above: Teignmouth Old Quay Signal Box guarded access to the busy docks that exported china clay extracted from the Teign Valley. Teignmouth station was (and remains) an ornate Italianate structure in cut stone that contrasts with the local red sandstone, and which must have been a source of great civic pride when built. The stonework extends westwards along the cutting walls so that this brick-built signal box (about 200 yards to the west of the station) appears out of place, unlike so many boxes that blended comfortably into their immediate surroundings. The 9.30 am Paddington – Falmouth & Newquay passes hauled by Castle Class No 5034 *Earl of Ducie* on 14th July 1958. *RCR 12261.*

Opposite top: Newton Abbot East Box stood in the V of the junction shortly before the mainline crossed the River Teign in the Exeter direction. The line diverging to the left allowed access to Newton Abbot Goods Yard, and also to the reasonably busy route to Heathfield which handled china clay shipments. Heathfield was a junction from where the Moretonhampstead branch pursued a north-westerly course while the Teign Valley route diverged northwards through Trusham and then eastwards by way of Longdown to re-connect with the main line close to Exeter docks. Before its severance in 1961, this route occasionally handled traffic diverted from the storm-threatened Dawlish Warren-Teignmouth section. There have been intermittent proposals since for its resuscitation to restore this function.

Back at Newton Abbot, Warship Class 42 No D805 *Benbow* is apparently departing light engine, possibly making for Hackney Goods Sidings on the down side of the mainline, just beyond the bridge. *RCR 13891.*

Opposite bottom: Newton Abbot West Signal Box was sited at the commencement of the West of England's final section of 4-road mainline that extended as far as Aller Junction, one mile to the west where the Torbay and Penzance routes part company. The Carriage & Wagon Works of the South Devon Railway was located in the large stone building behind the signal box and on the far side of the down lines. No 4940 *Ludford Hall* plus an unidentified Castle are passing to the rear of the box on the evening up mail service on 13th July 1959. No 4940 was an early Hall casualty being withdrawn the following November. *RCR 13858.*

NEWTON ABBOT WEST SIGNAL BOX
4940

Stratford-Upon-Avon Evesham Road Crossing was a modest affair that guarded the level crossing between Stratford-Upon-Avon Racecourse Station and the town's main station, but was no less essential in helping sustain the GWR's enviable reputation for safety, as reinforced by the ATC ramp in the foreground. ***RCR 17992.***

Opposite bottom: Liskeard Branch Signal Box stood at the entrance to the terminus section of Liskeard station whose platform is at a right angle to the mainline through platforms. Small prairie No 4552 is on a service from Looe which would have entailed reversal and run round at Coombe Junction in the Looe Valley before climbing the Liskeard loop to reach the terminus. The signalman is preparing to accept the token on 17th July 1960; this box also controlled the connection to the through station, the rails for which are to the right. The train is the usual mixture of stock comprising one of the ubiquitous C54 All Thirds of 1925 design, a later vintage (1930s) All Third and what appears to be a Brake Third of the 1920s. *RCR 15086.*

Above: St Dennis Junction Signal Box handled an unusual diversity of traffic for a rural location. West Cornwall was a mining region whose importance had stimulated the 19th Century construction of the Cornwall Minerals Railway. The CMR developed a network of 45 route miles plus numerous industrial sidings while also running passenger services between Newquay and Fowey; the enterprise was taken over by the GWR in 1896. At St Dennis Junction the line to Newquay from Par (on the Plymouth-Penzance route) connected with the ex-CMR freight only network that served various mining operations to the south.

The signal box stood adjacent to the Par-Newquay route on the left which saw heavy passenger traffic in the summer months. The industrial route which wended its way south eventually joining the GWR at Burngullow is on the right. On 11th July 1955, small prairie No 4526 is arriving with a train of china clay "hoods". The Toad immediately behind the locomotive suggests that having gained the Newquay route, and the engine will then run round before proceeding eastwards to Par. Perhaps the ultimate destination was Par Harbour where the load would be discharged for export.

On the right stands 0-6-0PT No 3635 which is apparently engaged in shunting the sidings where another hood is standing. The white mounds in the far distance are waste tips resulting from the extraction of china clay (kaolin). *RCR 6405.*

Opposite: Plymouth Mill Bay Signal Box on the inside. This was a busy establishment with a frame of 115 levers that worked to Cornwall Junction Signal Box around 400 yards to the north and to Millbay Crossing Signal Box rather more than a quarter of a mile to the south. This box was unusual in being a three-storey building with access to the mechanical interlocking through the middle floor. GWR signalmen were a breed apart, conscientious, dedicated and intensely proud of their work, as expressed in this cabin's immaculate condition. While many of the instruments on the block shelf date from GWR days, more modern 'light' indicators hanging below the shelf have either replaced the old or have been added to confirm the position/ indication of points and signals which are now electrically operated by switches worked from the shortened levers. ***RCR Ref unconfirmed.***

Above: Plymouth Mill Bay Signal Box on the outside. From April 1849, Plymouth Millbay Station served as the western terminus of the South Devon Railway but was reduced to a secondary role with the opening in 1877 of Plymouth North Road (about half a mile to the north-east) on the London-Penzance through route. Some services continued to terminate there while the nearby docks were integral to the transatlantic services that connected with GWR special trains for mails, and with those of the London & South Western for passengers.

His Majesty's Naval Dockyard at Devonport further west was a key target for the Luftwaffe during the Second World War and between July 1940 and May 1944, the city suffered fifty-nine night bombing raids. The dockyards were the main target but damage was sustained across the city. A population that had been 220,000 before the war was reduced to 127,000 at its lowest point. Civilian fatalities totalled 1,172 with 4,448 injured. Property damage included destruction of the two main shopping centres plus nearly every civic building, 26 schools, eight cinemas and 41 churches. A total of 3,754 houses were destroyed and a further 18,398 were seriously damaged. The GWR's Millbay station did not escape and was closed to all passenger services following its destruction in 1941.

Plymouth Mill Bay Signal Box (note different spelling) stood in the heart of the city to the east of the line from North Road to Millbay docks. Signalmen during the Blitz earned universal respect for their devotion to duty, remaining at their posts during the most adverse of conditions, and ever ready to provide verbal advice and warnings to engine crews as they crawled from box to box during the blackout.

Consider the calibre of those who faithfully worked through those terrible nights in a glass walled room that surmounted an elevated wooden structure. ***RCR 15695.***

Above: No 5915 *Trentham Hall* passes Old Oak Common East Signal Box on 8th August 1959 with an Up van train, probably for conveyance of parcels. This category of train often produced an interesting mixture of vehicles. In this case, the first is an inside-framed Siphon G, followed by a passenger brake van (apparently Diagram K41 or K42), and then one of the comparatively rare Siphons J. These differed from other bogie Siphons in using refrigeration (boxed iced) rather than fresh air ventilation to preserve the cargo. They were introduced in two batches in 1930 and 1934 but must have been soon superseded by the 6-wheel milk tank wagons that started to arrive in significant numbers from 1931-onwards.

The fourth vehicle is a BR General Utility Van as would seem is also the sixth. The fifth is apparently another GWR passenger brake van while bringing up the rear is a coach or possibly another PBV. No 5915 was one of the earliest Hall withdrawals, in January 1960. *RCR 14075.*

Below: Class 97xx 0-6-0PT No 9709 on a down train from Smithfield at Old Oak Common on 29th August 1959. Train composition was three containers on flats, six vans and a pair of Toad brake vans. A few 97s could be seen on local freight duties in the London area well into 1964. On the line behind the 97xx is bow -ended Composite Diagram E132 No W6091W (built July 1928, withdrawn December 1962), and to the right the third-class section of an all-maroon Sunshine coach of 1936/ 7 vintage with a droplight corridor window for every compartment where hitherto there would have been a full door. *RCR 14196.*

Chapter 8

Trains

In 1934, the Great Western introduced a system of reporting numbers to help train identification. The normal arrangement involved a 3-foot wide frame affixed to the smokebox door into which were slotted 20-inch high metal plates with white numbers on a black background. Their size made them readable up to about a quarter of a mile distant. Occasionally smaller plates with paper numbers pasted on were used, or the number was chalked or whitewashed on the door – quite effective provided that the weather stayed dry. For much of the year in areas where services were infrequent, the numbers were probably unnecessary but the system was invaluable at busy junctions and during peak times e.g. summer Saturdays. The arrangement continued into BR days but with the transfer of front numbers from the buffer beam to a cast iron number plate on the smokebox door, the class was still readily identifiable but the locomotive's specific identity was anonymous on approach.

The GWR's system underwent an extensive revision in 1951 to provide a more logical grouping of the numbers and was not revised again until the late 1959 which fortunately covers many trains that appear in this album. However, the numbers cannot be taken as gospel as while the general discipline remained, some individual numbers were amended year-to-year. Also, although the correct number should have been affixed during servicing for the next duty, this could be overlooked.

Well into the 1960s, Collett and Hawksworth stock still appeared among ubiquitous BR Mark 1s, in part substituting for waning interest in the modern, head end power. By deduction and analysis, it is often possible to work out at least part of the train's composition. Only a few non-passenger trains that offer points of operating interest are included in this volume. Perhaps brown vehicles and freight wagons will be the subject of later attention.

A suburban down train approaches Southall on 10th August 1957 hauled by 0-6-0PT Class 8750 No 9789. The five-coach rake is again a mixture. The first vehicle appears to be a Collett Brake Third (Diagram D125), followed by a pair of BR Mark 1s, then a Hawksworth 10-compartment Third (C83) and finally a Brake Third which judging by the body profile might be a bow-ended coach. *RCR 11067.*

Above: Prairie Class 61xx No 6157 accelerates a down Thames Valley local service past Old Oak Common East Signal Box on 29th August 1959. The 61s were built specially for suburban services out of Paddington and were regarded as a de lux version of Class 5101. Their boilers were to the same dimensions but manufactured from higher tensile nickel steel. Boiler pressure was 225 lbs/ sq in which raised the tractive effort to 27,340 lb. As these engines replaced ageing 2-4-0T Metros over electrified lines, they were equipped with trip gear to activate the brakes should a signal be passed at danger. Also, the ATC equipment automatically clipped up to avoid fouling the centre rail.

The GWR's designation system for fixed suburban/ non-corridor sets was confusing as consists varied from division to division and year to year. There appears to be no complete reference record of the designations used but suffice to say that the well-known B-set consisting of a pair of Brake composites was not a universal type as in at least two divisions before the war, B-sets officially comprised four coaches. In the London Division, there were at least the following set designations:- Suburban-set (4 coaches); 4-coach A-set; 5-coach A set; B-set (2 coaches); C-set (5); Local D-set (6); D-set (4); E-set (4); G -set (6); H-set (3). This list is probably incomplete but the closest designation applicable to No 6157's train would seem to be 5-coach A-set.

The consist is a mixture:- first coach is a BR Mark 1 suburban Brake Third (compartment section leading); the second is a Hawksworth 10 compartment 100-seater All Third (Diagram C83); the next seems to be a Hawksworth Composite; the fourth is another BR Mark 1; the end coach appears to be a GWR Brake Third. Scenes like this were on borrowed time as diesel multiple units started to take over Paddington's suburban services the following year. *RCR 14205.*

Opposite top: Hawksworth-designed 0-6-0PT Class 15xx No 1507 is about to cross the main lines by way of the flying junction with a Paddington-bound empty stock train from Old Oak Common carriage sidings on 17th April 1960. These sturdy engines were popular for hauling empty trains to and from the terminus. *RCR 8245.*

Opposite bottom: No 5003 *Lulworth Castle* on a down express at Iver on 27th May 1956 *RCR 7298.*

5003

144

This page: 2-6-0 Class 43xx was Churchward's largest class, in numerical terms. They were genuine mixed traffic engines but appearances on passenger services into Paddington by the mid-1950s would have been rare. The train reporting number displayed by No 7317 on 7th July 1956 as it passed through Tilehurst suggests that this was an inter-regional working bound for the Southern. The locomotive might provide a clue regarding destination as being a 2-6-0 on the Up Slow, it would gain the Southern at Reading and proceed on to Redhill or the South East. At Tilehurst, a train destined for Southampton/ Bournemouth via Basingstoke would more likely be in the hands of a Hall or Grange and on the Up Main, to minimise conflicting traffic movements when taking the west curve at Reading. *RCR 7457.*

Opposite top: Sonning Cutting has appeared many times as the setting for GWR trains and no album would be complete without an image like this of No *6003 King George IV* on 7th July 1956. Train No 144 was the 11.30 am Paddington-CR Penzance (Monday to Fridays) which on Saturdays terminated at Minehead. *RCR 7453.*

Opposite bottom: Class 56xx No 5697 on an Up freight at Sonning Cutting on 19th May 1956. This class is indelibly associated with South Wales but in the mid-1950s, around ten were allocated to the London Division. *RCR 7229.*

Above: BR "Britannia" Class 4-6-2 No 70026 *Polar Star* on "The Red Dragon" bound for London and passing Coalpit Heath on 20th September 1955. These pacifics gained early acceptance on other regions but were unpopular at first on the Western, possibly due to prejudice rather than any particular design defect. However, once concentrated on South Wales services, they put in good work. Much of this 13-coach train appears to be a matched set of late Collett coaches, marred at the leading end by the earlier vintage Brake Third. *RCR 6836.*

Opposite bottom: BR Class 5 4-6-0 No 73029 is approaching Oxford from the north with a Weymouth-bound train on 15th August 1959. Behind the ex-LMS passenger brake vehicle, the stock appears to be all ex-GWR. Continuing south this train will take the Didcot East Curve to follow the Bristol-Paddington main line as far as Reading where it will reach the Berks & Hants line by means of the West Curve. Its route thereafter is uncertain as it would have the option of crossing to the ex-LSWR route at Basingstoke by way of Southcote Junction, or of continuing down the ex-GWR West of England main line and branching off at Castle Cary. *RCR 14084.*

Right: No 7015 *Carn Brea Castle* picks up water from Aldermaston troughs while working the 1.15 pm Saturdays only Paignton-Paddington on 7th July 1956. By this time regular express services comprised largely BR Mark 1 coaches, except for catering vehicles, but the Saturday "extras" could see employment of older rolling stock and this train is no exception. The locomotive is almost exactly eight years old but several of the coaches are decidedly older. The first and second coaches are Centenary Stock, a Brake Composite (diagram E150) followed by a Composite (E149) (third class compartments leading). The third vehicle is a Toplight Brake Third (its age reflected in the evidence of sag in the body) while the next two are much younger being Hawksworth coaches of similar vintage to the locomotive. The sixth seems to be a pre-Sunshine Collett Composite; the likely identities of the remainder cannot be discerned but there is a distinct Great Western flavour to the whole eleven vehicle rake. *RCR 7467.*

THE RAILWAY HOTEL
2240

5385

This page: On 14th May 1955, 43xx Class No 6341 was shunting wagons from its train at Ludgershall on the ex-Midland & South Western Joint Railway route from Andoversford (near Cheltenham) that connected with Andover on the ex-London & South Western Railway main line. This was an area that saw much military traffic with Ludgershall serving as the junction for the Tidworth branch, which can be seen branching off in the left foreground. The double-face platform in the yard was installed in 1898 to handle troop trains but does not appear to have been used for that purpose for a number of years. Other details include the military Nissen huts in the left background, the grounded coach body at the yard entrance which appears to be an ex-GWR 4-wheeler, and the tall home signals installed to the right of the running lines presumably to improve sighting in connection with the road overbridge. *RCR 6106.*

Opposite top: On 7th July 1956 Class 2251 0-6-0 No 2240 stands in the Up platform loop at Newbury awaiting passage of a train signalled through on the Up main. No 6910 *Gossington Hall* is arriving at the down platform with a troop train that presumably started out from somewhere in the north and travelled by way of Oxford and Reading west loop to reach here. The purpose of the pause at Newbury would appear to be for personal comfort as the first four coaches are BR Mark 1 non-corridor suburbans; officers and NCOs no doubt rode in the gangwayed stock to the rear. *RCR 7469.*

Opposite bottom: Churchward Mogul No 5385 appears to be leaving Newbury on a local working (Hawksworth Brake Third leading) on 7th July 1956. However, Dick Riley describes this as a shunting movement. Perhaps the train is drawing forward to reverse into the bay to collect what appears to be a horse box. On the Didcot, Newbury and Southampton route it was normal operating practice to collect/detach vans and horse boxes in this fashion. *RCR 7471.*

Left: Castle Class No 5058 *Beaufort* has cleared the tunnel and is cruising past Whiteball Siding Signal Box on 4th September 1954 with the 7.43 am Nottingham-Plymouth. The train is comprised of ex-LMS stock, the first, second and fifth coaches being Period III while the third and fourth are of earlier vintage. Built as *Lamphey Castle* in May 1939, No 5078 was renamed in January 1941 to recognise aircraft that had become household names during the Battle of Britain. Twelve castles in the 5071-5082 series were so honoured. *RCR 5443.*

Bottom: Churchward Class 43xx No 6358 stands at Tiverton Junction on 27th July 1958. The 0-4-2T Class 14xx that worked the shuttle from the junction to Tiverton can just be glimpsed behind. Brake Third No W4122W is from the first batch of "Sunshine Stock" (Diagram D121) introduced in 1936, now relegated to secondary duties. It was withdrawn in 1963 together with the remainder of that diagram. *RCR 12471.*

Right: The sea wall at Teignmouth was a favourite spot for photographers. On 14th July 1959, a family group stopped to admire the passage of No 5005 *Manorbier Castle*. This locomotive was partially streamlined in 1935 (together with King No 6014) but removal of the various fittings commenced later that year and proceeded in piecemeal fashion until 1946/ 7. The only special feature remaining at withdrawal in February 1960 was the snifting valve set just above the inside cylinder covers. The train is unidentified but the coaching stock is ex-LMS.

A few yards behind the photographer the line curves to the right and inland towards Teignmouth station. Looking towards Dawlish, in the middle distance is Sprey Point, the section of sea wall surrounding a square of land that juts into the sea. In the far distance can be seen the exhaust of an up train about to enter Parson's Tunnel, at 513 yards the longest of the five tunnels in the section to Dawlish. *RCR 13864.*

Another view of the sea wall at Teignmouth, this time from an unusual angle as "The Devonian" hauled by No 5032 *Usk Castle* passes under the lofty bridge that carries Eastcliff Walk over the railway on 18th July 1958. The approach signal is placed well away from the trackside to help sighting on the curve and with typical GWR thoroughness concerning safety, the ATC ramp is alongside in the four foot. When built by the South Devon Railway, this stretch was in the Eastcliff Tunnel. However, in 1884 the GWR opened it out to form a deep cutting, requiring construction of the bridge. *RCR 12332.*

Having surmounted the sharp gradients up to the "spike" at Dainton Tunnel, the remaining challenge for Paddington-Plymouth services was Rattery Bank. The crossing of the River Dart and the run through Totnes station is on the level at an elevation as low as any on the entire route to Penzance, followed by a climb over nine miles to the highest point west of Savernake. Immediately beyond Totnes station, the bank starts at 1 in 66, and the worst gradients are over the next four miles including sections at 1 in 46, 47 and 50. Large prairie No 4109, probably one of Newton Abbot's banker allocation, is setting to work helping a goods train on its way to Plymouth on 18th July 1956. Immediately in front of the locomotive is 20-ton Toad Brake Van No W 35933 (Diagram AA23 built 1942-9).

The engine has just passed the low headroom bridge over the side road quaintly named "Malt Mill". Totnes had two through lines and two platform line roads; the down platform and adjacent bay can be seen under the overbridge that carries the main road to Ashburton. The station was an important loading point for the dairy that was on the Up side, sandwiched between the station and the river Dart, hidden in this view by the houses to the left of the road bridge. A milk tanker can be seen on the siding beside the Up line.

The main line is on a sharp curve to the left at this point which accounts for the Up approach signal gantry standing well off to the right. ***RCR 7712***

On 14th July 1956, No 5996 *Mytton Hall* piloted No 6016 *King Edward V* on the climb of Hemerdon Bank with the Saturdays Only 8.15 am Perranporth-Paddington. The worst part of this bank was two miles at 1 in 42 which started to the east of Plympton, around six miles from Plymouth North Road. Thereafter, the eight miles or so climb to the summit at Wrangaton was much gentler. Hemerdon was very likely regarded as the least fearsome of the four south Devon banks as fresh crews and engines would come on at North Road, and because the six-mile stretch before the climb was enough for the motive power to be thoroughly "warmed up". Nevertheless, the two locomotives are putting in maximum effort in a picture that sums up all the drama of moving heavy steam trains through south Devon. The Hall would have come off at Newton Abbot as it was photographed by Dick Riley later that day piloting No 6012 *King Edward VI* near Tigley Signal Box on the climb of Rattery Bank with the Saturdays Only 11.00 am Paddington-Penzance.

Four of the first five coaches are BR Mark 1 vehicles while the remainder seem to be ex-GWR, apparently including a catering vehicle. Among the Mark1s, the second coach is therefore interesting as it is of GWR origin and running on 4-wheel bogies. It seems to be a 71' 4" bow-ended Composite Diner of either Diagram H26 or H29. *RCR 7629.*

Top: Plympton is an ancient town, mentioned in the Domesday Book, which became a north-eastern suburb of the city of Plymouth in 1967. The South Devon Railway opened the station in 1848 which from 1st June 1904 became the eastern terminus for up-graded suburban services in the Plymouth area. Rationalisation saw its closure on 3rd March 1959 as part of a programme that removed several stations in the greater Plymouth area, despite their potential as part of the city's modern commuter network.

The date is 15th July 1958 and No 6858 *Woolston Grange* pilots No 5098 *Clifford Castle* on what is described in Riley's notes as the 5.30 am from Paddington (reporting No 100). This was a train of some notoriety whose journey from London to Penzance via Bristol included many stops *en route.* This service was a survivor of the "parliamentary" system initiated under the Railway Regulation Act of 1844 and judging by the shadows, it must be early afternoon. Any long-suffering passenger who had boarded at Paddington still had a way to go as this train would crawl into Penzance around 4.00 pm. *RCR 12273.*

Bottom: Milk for London was an important source of traffic. Traditionally it had travelled from farm to railway loading point in churns for transfer into milk vans, latterly usually bogie Siphons G. Four-wheeled tank wagons were introduced in 1927 but being unstable at speed, they had all been replaced by 6-wheelers before the war. By the time Dick Reilly was photographing trains on the move, virtually all milk had graduated to tankers and the useful Siphons had moved to general utility duties.

Milk was shipped in dedicated trains consisting of a rake of tankers plus a passenger brake van, and were memorable for haulage by large locomotives – Castles, Halls, Counties, Granges, 47xx etc. This was necessary as 6-wheel tank wagons had a tare weight of around 13 to 14 tons with a tank capacity of 3000 gallons. Fully laden the all up weight was roughly doubled i.e. the approximate equivalent of a fully loaded mainline passenger carriage.

On 7th July 1955, the 6.20 pm milk train from Penzance had reached Dalcoath milk siding about half a mile east of Camborne. No 1018 *County of Leicester* is in process of collecting a tanker to add to its load. The remainder of the train with a passenger brake van on the rear is standing on the main line; the running number cannot be discerned but this vehicle appears to be a Collett Diagram K41. *RCR 5772.*

The 12.20 pm Penzance milk is passing Laira Junction Signal Box on 13th July 1956 in the hands of Class 78xx No 7809 *Childrey Manor* as pilot and Class 2884 No 3845. This train composition appears to be 13 tankers plus passenger brake van plus another tanker and finally a pair of Cordon gas tank wagons, presumably being returned empty. This would have produced an aggregated train load of 420-440 tons.

While the train is the main focus, this photograph contains a wealth of detail which includes:- the 4' gauge Lee Moor tramway crossing in the foreground; the plethora of signals (including that which controls the tramway's admission to the crossing); the rather cramped carriage sidings to the right (where Saltash service auto trailers were often parked); the intricate slips that allowed access to those sidings; the further Cordons standing to the far right; Laira MPD in the far distance, partially hidden by a cloud of steam and a haze of smoke; the further stock stored in the sidings to the far right. *RCR 7621.*

Top: Milk from the West Country was discharged at the Milk Marketing Board depot at Kensington Olympia and the empties were then worked back to staging points as the first phase of the return journey. This train, consisting of four tankers, what appears to be a Fruit C, a passenger brake van, and then another six tankers is on its way southwards down the West Ealing Loop. Dick Riley photographed this working later that day as 0-6-0PT No 9708 stowed its train in sidings at West Ealing.

This working would have followed a circuitous route to reach this point. The empties would have returned back up the West London line to North Pole Junction and then over the Victoria Branch to the Paddington-Bristol Down Slow, before branching off at Old Oak Common on to the Acton and Northolt line. The train would have then proceeded through North Acton, Park Royal and Perivale before taking the east curve immediately before Greenford on to the West Ealing Loop. This course minimised conflicting movements over the Paddington-Bristol route. *RCR Ref unconfirmed.*

Broccoli was another of Cornwall's important agricultural products that was shipped to London. As a seasonal crop, purpose-designed vehicles could not be justified so surplus cattle wagons were used on this service. Here small prairie Class 45xx No 4564 is shunting a rake of such wagons loaded with the vegetable at Gwinear Road on 9th April 1960. *RCR 14647.*

Opposite bottom: Returning for more, No 7812 *Erlestoke Manor* stands at Truro on a down train that includes two empty milk vehicles at its head. The first is a six-wheeler flat wagon with a road tanker aboard for transit of milk (ie operating on roll-on, roll-off basis). The second is a conventional 6-wheel milk tanker followed by a Passenger Brake Van, and then closed vans. The picture shows how interesting was the railway in those days – the Cordon at the buffer stops, the other wagons in the background, the array of signals, the B-Set standing in the Falmouth bay to the right – all far removed from today's "antiseptic" atmosphere and "bus-stop" architecture. *RCR Ref unconfirmed.*

This page, bottom: Truro on 20th July 1960 with evidence that the transition to diesel power is gathering momentum. The modestly-powered D63xx "baby Warships" frequently worked in tandem when working mainline trains; Nos D6327 and possibly D6309 stand in the loop on the left. Laira's No 5029 *Nunney Castle* is at the Down platform, heading a train of rather mixed stock. The first is a Period III LMS vehicle, the second a GW Passenger Brake Van (apparently of Diagram K40), the third's origins cannot be determined, and the fourth is a Hawksworth coach. *RCR 15162.*

This page: On 5th July 1955, Dick Riley visited Princetown, terminus of the branch from Yelverton on the Marsh Mills, Plymouth to Launceston route and at 1430 ft, the highest railway station in England. In the first view, small prairie No 4410 is near Ingra Tor Halt with a mixed train comprising a Brake Composite, two vans and a Toad. The second view shows the same train approaching the terminus. The third depicts the return journey towards Yelverton with just the coach, the engine having been turned on the 23' 6" turntable at Princetown. Sharp bends and steep gradients made the branch difficult to work and a 44xx prairie with 4' 1½" driving wheels was the preferred motive power. No 4410 was withdrawn in September 1955; the branch line was closed on 3rd March 1956. *RCR 6246, 6257, 6258.*

Opposite top: Class 4575 2-6-2T No 5535 approaches Tavistock Junction near Plymouth with a goods train on 11th July 1956. *RCR 7596.*

Opposite bottom: Plymouth, Laira Junction again with double -chimney No 6016 *King Edward V* passing the signal box on 15th July 1958 on the up "Royal Duchy" Penzance-Paddington service. *RCR 12279.*

THE ROYAL DUCHY

Above: On 5th July 1963 Class 45xx 2-6-2T No 4555 was in charge of a Booth-Rodley built engineering crane, match truck, two vans and LMS-style brake van just east of Laira Junction, beside the River Plym. *RCR 17213.*

On 30th August 1954, 0-6-0PT No 9655 was in charge of three coaches and a van forming a Par-Newquay train at Middleway Crossing Signal Box. The ubiquitous pannier has a load comprising a Hawksworth Diagram C 84 All third, plus a Collett flat-ended All Third of either Diagram C65 or C67, and finally a Churchward -era Toplight brake coach (unfortunately too distant for more specific definition) – three generations of classic GWR vehicles. *RCR 5942.*

Chapter 9

Auto trains

Around the turn of the century the railways' suburban services started to suffer the competitive impact of the electric tramcar. In response, several companies introduced steam rail motors (SRMs) where a coach and a small steam locomotive were combined to form a self-propelled unit. The concept found a certain favour with the commuting public and to some extent arrested the migration from rail to tram. The Great Western took up the idea with enthusiasm, eventually deploying a fleet of 99 SRMs.

It is surprising that so many were built as operational limitations soon became apparent. A steam locomotive takes longer to service than does a coach so reducing the latter's revenue-earning availability. Maintenance usually took place in a locomotive depot where the environment complicated the cleaning of the passenger accommodation. The locomotive's size was limited by the need to maximise passenger seating, necessitating a small vertical boiler that was difficult to fire. SRMs' commercial success often stimulated growth in custom that demanded attachment of a trailer vehicle thereby unduly stretching the power unit's haulage capacity.

The solution to divide the coach from the locomotive unit, and to substitute a small "push-pull" equipped conventional tank engine for the latter was simple and effective. Different maintenance regimes could be adopted, the coach could be used more intensively, and the locomotive could be deployed on other duties. Thus was born the archetypal auto train which as much as the 4-6-0 and 2-8-0 locomotive fleets characterised the old Great Western well into the nationalisation period.

Previous page: The classic motive power for single coach auto trains from the mid-1930s onwards was 0-4-2T Class 48xx (later re-designated Class 14xx). On 27th February 1954, No 1420 has arrived at Oxford General with a service from Blenheim and Woodstock. It is decorated with chalked messages on its tank and cab sides including "Cheerio", "R.I.P" and "Born 1890, Nationalised 1948, ??? 27/2/54" for this was the last day of services over that branch. *RCR 5014.*

Above: The same train arriving a little earlier at Oxford General. No 1420's companion started life as SRM No 84 in December 1907 and was withdrawn in March 1930. The coach portion was then used to create Auto Trailer No 183. In this form as Diagram A26, its leading dimensions were 70' long by 9' wide, with seating for 77 third-class passengers and weighing 32 tons. The trailer was withdrawn in October 1954 whereas No 1420 worked until October 1964, and was then preserved. *RCR 5013.*

Opposite top: The early SRMs (Nos 1 to 14, 17 to 28) had rather stark flat-sided matchboard bodies that contrasted with the ornate panelled conventional coaching stock of the Edwardian era. This styling was retained when the engine portion was removed and the coach was converted to auto trailer. This vehicle had started life as SRM No 12 under Diagram D in June 1904 and was withdrawn in December 1915. The coach portion re-emerged as Diagram A7 Trailer No 110 exactly a year later in which condition it carried 58 third class passengers in its 59' 6" by 8' 6" body.

Withdrawn September 1953, No 110 was photographed on 14th May 1951 standing in the siding at Abingdon beside the Maltings and the Gas Works, which was the habitual parking place for the branch's spare trailer. If brought into use at short notice, it was unpopular for the stale, musty atmosphere that pervaded the two saloons. *RCR 2232.*

The last matchboard-bodied SRM built was No 28 in September 1904 (Diagram G – 59' by 8' 6" body). It ceased work in September 1916 but its coach portion did not emerge as Trailer No 124 (Diagram A9) until February 1920. When photographed with its retractable passenger steps extended at Caerphilly on 15th May 1952, it was nearing the end of its life as withdrawal came in October 1953. *RCR 3480.*

Top: Purpose-built auto trailers, as opposed to the SRM conversions, were first introduced in December 1903. A total of 30 were built to Diagram L in the 1906-8 period being the most numerous type to appear under GWR auspices. They had 70' by 9' bodies carried on a variety of bogies including the 9' American type seen here, and were equipped with gangway connections at the non-driving end. They seated 76 third class passengers and were widely distributed throughout the system. All remained in service until the 1950s.

No W60W had been repainted in plain maroon livery, its toplights plated over and numbers applied in the 1951-style by the time of its withdrawal in March 1958. A few of Diagram L were retained for departmental-type duties and this vehicle was effectively grounded (albeit with bogies and wheels intact) to provide staff and/ office accommodation at Laira when photographed on 27th August 1961. *RCR 16168.*

Opposite bottom: Trailer No W161W of Diagram A27 appeared in December 1928 in the first batch of new auto coaches to be built since 1912. In the interim, additional needs were met by SRM conversions and by vehicles inherited from other companies at the Grouping.

Trailers in this diagram were the first with steel body panels over the traditional timber frame, and with electric lighting. The retractable passenger steps for use at halts with low level platforms were retained although whether this feature was still needed must have been questionable. Toplights which had not been applied in new coach construction for several years were reintroduced, hinged for ventilation purposes. The overall dimensions were 59' 6" by 9' and seating accommodation for 72 third class passengers was provided. No W161W, withdrawn in July 1959, is standing at Laira with the new diesel depot then under construction in the background. ***RCR reference not confirmed.***

Below: The enduring nature of GWR design and practice is typified in this well-known view of Class 14xx No 1470 crossing the River Dart near Buckfastleigh with the 12.18 pm Totnes-Ashburton service on 17th July 1956. There were 75 of this type that derived from the more numerous Class 517 of 1868.

The trailer is No W244W of Diagram A43, one of 25 built by BR Western Region in the 1951-4 period to replace older examples then at the end of their working lives. The new vehicles were steel-bodied and built to modern standards including BR-type windows, with a body length of 63' which had not been used before. Beyond that, they were entirely traditional in concept and layout (except that Nos W220 and W221 were named *Thrush* and *Wren* respectively). No 244 was the last purpose-built trailer to be introduced to service. No 1470 very much belongs in this picture as for many years it was the regular locomotive on the Ashburton auto services. ***RCR 7708.***

In contrast to rural byways, the auto train filled a vital suburban role in the Plymouth area in breaching the natural barrier of the River Tamar. Before the suspension bridge to Saltash opened in 1962, motor traffic aiming for eastern Cornwall had the choice of either the slow and busy Torpoint Ferry near Devonport, or the lowest bridge over the river at Gunnislake. The latter, which dated from 1520, is roughly 10 miles to the north of Plymouth as the crow flies but significantly further by the circuitous road network. The rail service between the city and Saltash was thus an important transport link.

Saltash station is on a cramped and awkward site which meant that trains terminated and reversed on the mainline, an operating practice for which auto trains were ideally suited. Trailers of Diagrams Q (80 seats) and R (84 seats) which appeared in 1909/ 1912 were primarily intended for Saltash services, although they occasionally appeared elsewhere in the West Country. There were five of each type, Diagram Q being driving trailers while R were intermediates, with gangway connections between. The 1912 batch were the last 70' timber panelled, purpose-built trailers to be introduced. They are thought to have worked in pairs throughout their careers, and the Saltash services from the 1930s onwards typically comprised two pairs with an 0-6-0PT Class 64xx in between. This driver's view of the Royal Albert Bridge from a train that has just departed Saltash is dated 13th July 1956. The vehicle is unidentified but there were three each of Diagrams Q and R still in service so this might be the driving cab of one of the trailers Nos 93 to 95. Crossing the bridge was a cautious affair as witness the fixed distant signal. ***RCR Ref unconfirmed.***

Afterword

Accuracy: Every reasonable effort has been made to ensure that the Riley Collection reference quoted with each caption is correct for the relative image portrayed. The caption information specific to the image (subject matter, location and date) is based on the photographer's personal records and where deemed necessary has been cross-checked with third party reference sources. It should be noted that in some cases the photographer's records relating to some images are non-existent or incomplete. Also, precise definition might have been compromised by the collection containing a series of photographs concentrated on a specific subject taken at the same location on the same date.

The Cameras: Dick Riley's first railway photograph was of LNER No 4473 *Solario* departing Kings Cross and by his own admission, it was a disaster that proved his Box Brownie was not up to the task. Progress was made with a Kodak folding camera acquired in 1937 but its shutter speed of 1/100 precluded moving trains. After the war, a Zeiss Ikonta with a speed of 1/250 led to a wider range of subjects and better results.

However, he felt that his work did not mature until 1954 when he started to do his own developing and printing, which coincided with his joining Maurice Earley's Railway Photographic Society. By then he was successfully tackling a broad range of subjects. Holidays were largely devoted to photographing railways, and he usually took a roll film developer with him. His favoured combination was Ilford FP3 film with a Promicrol developer.

In 1955, he purchased second-hand an Agfa Isolette with a speed of 1/500, followed by an Agfa Record 3 that gave 2¼" by 3¼" negatives rather than 2¼" square. Also in 1954, he started to take colour transparencies but was hampered by a lens of f3.5 and slow Kodachrome 8 ASA film that again prevented photographing moving trains. This was rectified in 1957 with an Agfa Silette with f2 lens. In 1967, by which time his railway-related activities had all but ceased, he acquired a Canon SLR f1.8. Dick Riley asserted that he never paid more than £20 for a camera for black and white photography.

The Car: Some photographic sequences show that on occasions, Dick Riley rode in the first vehicle of stopping trains and alighted at each pause to photograph the locomotive. The rear three-quarter views of Nos 9017 (page 21) and 4705 (page 23) were taken in this fashion. As his work expanded to embrace the train and the railway in a variety of locations, road transport became as essential a part of the mission as were the cameras.

As revealed in some of the photographs, Morris Minor Tourer Registration No YHX 757 (a London number) was the means of getting about. The car was either a later-built Series 1 with headlights in the raised position and a 918-cc side valve engine of pre-war design or (more likely) a Series 2 with a more modern 803-cc overhead valve engine. This version had a top speed of 63 mph and could accelerate from 0 to 60 mph in a breath-taking 52 seconds.

Acknowledgements: Thanks to the Publisher for agreeing to bring this work to print; to the Editor whose guiding hand, patience and forbearance has been tested and not found wanting; and to Amyas Crump whose encyclopaedic route knowledge has solved thorny questions regarding certain locations.

Bibliography:

A G Atkins, W Beard, R Tourret. 'GWR Goods Wagons.' OPC 2013.
Jeremy Clements. 'William Dean: The greatest of them all.' Noodle Books 2012.
R A Cooke. 'Atlas of the Great Western Railway as at 1947.' Wild Swan Publications 1988.
Michael Harris. 'Great Western Coaches from 1890.' David & Charles 1985.
John Lewis. 'Great Western Auto Trailers Part 1. Wild Swan Publications 1991.
John Lewis. 'Great Western Auto Trailers Part 2. Wild Swan Publications 1995.
Hugh Longworth. 'British Railways Pre-Nationalisation Coaching Stock Vol 1.' OPC 2018.
E Lyons. 'An Historical Survey of Great Western Engine Sheds 1947'. OPC 1972.
Railway Correspondence & Travel Society. 'The Locomotives of the Great Western Railway.' 1951 et seq.
JH Russell. 'Great Western Wagons Appendix'. OPC 1974.

A view that sums up Dick Riley's search for rural trains so characteristic of the old Great Western. On a sunny summer's day, he has parked his Morris beside a quiet country road to capture the passage of 0-6-0PT Class 54xx No 5402 with an auto trailer at Keinton Mandeville bound for Castle Cary on 2nd July 1955. This class, which had 5' 2" driving wheels was introduced in 1930 specifically for auto services. The concept was expanded with 40 of Class 64xx built 1932-7 which were similar but with 4' 7½" driving wheels. The trailer is a purpose-built 70' Diagram U vehicle of which twelve numbered 81 to 92 were built August-September 1912. They were withdrawn 1955-8 except for No 91 which might have survived into the early 1960s. No 92 was rescued from departmental duties for preservation. ***RCR 6190.***